Excellence in Education
Series Editor: Dr Mark Brundrett

Excellence in the Teaching of English to Primary School Children

About this series

The series, *Excellence in Education*, draws on the expertise of both university academics and practitioners in highly successful schools. It is designed to offer practical strategies for school improvement underpinned by a rigorous examination of the theoretical perspectives upon which any such developments should be based. Teachers, advisers, university lecturers and those engaged in study for higher degrees or national professional development programmes will find the series to be both professionally relevant and intellectually stimulating.

Series Editor: Dr Mark Brundrett, University of Leicester

Other books in the series

The Beacon School Experience: case studies in excellence
edited by Mark Brundrett and Neil Burton

The Primary School Curriculum: developing effective teaching
edited by Mark Brundrett, Diane Duncan and Peter Silcock

The Beacon Schools Experience: developing the curriculum
edited by Neil Burton and Mark Brundrett

Excellence in the Teaching of English to Primary School Children

Edited by Diane Duncan,
Mark Brundrett and Peter Silcock

Peter Francis Publishers

Peter Francis Publishers
The Old School House
Little Fransham
Dereham
Norfolk NR19 2JP UK

© Diane Duncan, Mark Brundrett and Peter Silcock 2002

A CIP catalogue record for this book
is available from the British Library

ISBN 1-870167-39-2

Printed and bound in Great Britain by Biddles Ltd,
Guildford and King's Lynn.

Contents

Introduction

Diane Duncan

What do we mean by excellence in the teaching of English?

The aim of this book is to explore the complexity and diversity involved in the project of achieving excellence in the teaching of English. However, because each of the contributors has a particular response to how best that may be accomplished the book does not offer a fully worked out programmatic statement. We note that the DfEE (1997) gives no clear statement about what it means by excellence. This book then contains no manifesto which articulates a party line or puts a particular spin on excellence, although the contentious issue of the politicization of English is taken up later in this introduction.

How the book is organised

The first four chapters deal with aspects of literature, drama and poetry which include lesson plans and specific ideas for practice. Halfway through the book, at Chapter 6, is an account of how newly appointed curriculum leaders in English can get a foothold on the complex task of leading English. Chapters 7 and 8 focus on specific aspects of knowledge about language; bilingualism and genre approaches to literacy. These chapters combine theoretical discourse with some sharply focused classroom application, which draw upon the respective authors' research. The book ends with a chapter on how English can be taught through history. It offers some real possibilities of how English and history might be integrated provided there is substantial subject knowledge of both subjects. It is also a reminder of how the Bullock Report's (1975) ideal for language to be taught across the curriculum could be realised.

Each of the authors in this book has been selected to write chapters on specific aspects of teaching English because in my view they are all excellent teachers. It should be made clear however that their work as teacher educators is almost as constrained by the bureaucracy of the National Curriculum as that of school teachers. Yet despite that they all, without doubt, believe in what they do, care passionately about their subject or particular aspect of English and want to communicate their knowledge and enthusiasm in the most compelling way possible. They all have long experience of teaching children but they have also taught or are currently teaching student teachers, teachers and a range of adult learners.

For the purposes of this book however, the focus is upon teaching children. With two exceptions, I have seen all of them teach and what they each have in common is an ability to 'light' up and energise the minds of those they teach. The light they bring to their work is drawn from a rich source of dynamic subject knowledge. It is dynamic because they are constantly questioning and reflecting on what they know and teach. Its dynamic force comes partly from what they continue to learn from the experience of teaching and partly from what they learn through their reading, research and interaction with communities of English teachers and researchers at courses and conferences. Their particular interaction between practice and thought in its broadest sense is always seeking answers to new questions in ways which will lead to improved teaching. These teachers actively *listen* to what their learners tell them.

This may sound obvious but I am talking about the kind of intense and engaged listening which normally requires the mind to be still and quiet; we can only listen with quiet, attentive minds when we are confident and secure about what and how we are teaching. This kind of 'higher order' listening is rare in teaching because the range of demands on our minds and senses is usually too great to allow our minds to be quietly receptive. We also have to be prepared to suspend temporarily our teaching plan in order to allow new information to interact with our thinking. This new information may well challenge aspects of our teaching or something we have done or said in a particular lesson but we are sufficiently confident in our knowledge and self-belief that we can afford to take risks and respond to new ideas and questions we may not previously have thought about. In Chapter 1 Sedgwick makes this point succinctly: 'We are poor educators if we are not alert to the moving edge, which is always on the point of risk.' These questions and ideas become a source for further thought and reflection which, over a period of time, becomes another layer of knowledge which, in turn, feeds into the next lesson in the form of changes and modifications. This kind of recursive thinking at a number of levels keeps teaching material fresh, in touch with learners' needs in a constantly evolving dynamic between practice and reflection and teachers and learners. To put it another way, the teacher-authors in this book are able to 'read' accurately what children say and demonstrate in their learning behaviour and make instructive use of it in future teaching sessions.

Values and beliefs

Other sources of light which the writers in this book bring to their work are the beliefs and values which they hold about the teaching of English and the children they teach. Self-evidently they all want children to experience success and make tangible progress in their learning. What is distinctive about their teaching is the kind of choices they make about the content and materials they use and the way in which they engage children in the interface between ideas, concepts, skills, understanding and the part they play in taught sessions. Particular choices about the material they decide to use with children are based on a sharply focused understanding of how children learn, along with materials and ideas which they know are likely to enthuse and connect with children's interest and imagination. This knowledge of what is likely to work with children comes from experience and a preparedness to experiment and take risks. Clearly this means that some sessions are written off as experience but in the process learning takes place, which results in closer approximations to the match with children's interests and abilities.

The selection of some of the texts, poems, and ideas used by the authors in this book may surprise readers for their sophistication and what may, at first sight, appear to be inaccessible to primary school children. The use of extracts from Shakespeare's *Coriolanus* in Chapter 1; Alfred, Lord Tennyson's *The Lady of Shalott* in Chapter 3 and Dickens' *Great Expectations* in Chapter 4 are examples of texts which might normally be considered as more suitable for a secondary school rather than a primary school English curriculum. However, in each case the texts have been used selectively (sometimes just one line or word is used as a focus), to encourage children to think differently, using unfamiliar language to explore a familiar theme or situation within their own experience. It is the way this material is both structured and de-constructed for teaching and learning purposes which is distinctive and novel.

However, the content, structure and organisation of some of the lessons presented in this book is only part of the story as far as excellence is concerned. What is at least of equal significance are the writers' values about children as learners. All the authors respect the integrity of children's responses to teaching and see them as active and constructive learners who have a reciprocal relationship both with the content of the lesson and with those who teach them. Teachers and learners give as well as receive in the interaction which takes place in the classroom. The important point about their work is that whilst the teacher plays a leading, and interventionist, role in the pace and framing of the lesson, their interaction with children allows them to take some responsibility for their own learning. Such teachers take children's contributions seriously, accord them status in relation to the learning intentions of the lesson and, where possible, incorporate them into a learning experience for all pupils. In an autobiographical account of his career as an English teacher, roughly half a century ago and several decades before the introduction of the National Curriculum and the National Literacy Strategy Framework for Teaching, Barnes (2000: 98-9) wrote something similar on the role of the teacher and the value of group discussion as a precursor to writing:

> I had no doubt that the teacher's role is crucial, for it is he or she who must set up the opportunities for learning, provide frameworks that will shape and direct it, and encourage reflective understanding of new experiences and ideas … My own practice was based on the assumption that pupils need to borrow from the teacher and to have the opportunity to think and solve problems for themselves …

Beyond the confines of specific lessons, the authors want longer-term benefits for the children they teach. Of course they want children to enjoy and find pleasure in the power of language and the richness of written, visual and pictorial texts; but they also want children to learn to be critical, reflective and appreciative at the level of the imagination and emotions as well as the intellect. These qualities and abilities hold the potential to change and transform individuals in ways which may have a lifelong impact. This may sound hopelessly idealistic, especially in the current context of a heavily prescribed and target-driven curriculum but the teaching of English has always meant far more to its teachers than the provision of a curriculum for literacy.

Readers must judge for themselves what value systems pertain in the chapters of this book but a notable feature of its authors and all those teachers who continue to bring life and vigour to their work with children is their ability to hold true to their beliefs and convictions about the teaching of English in the face of one of the most politically driven and vehemently contested periods in the history of English teaching. Teachers who succeed in sustaining their value position in relation to both the subject itself and the children they have taught succeed in doing so throughout a period of intense political hostility towards teachers and academics who made valiant attempts to defend the original 'Cox' curriculum of 1989 (DES, 1989).

In a book which sets out to examine and present what it considers to be 'excellent' in the teaching of English, it is worth calling to mind some of the extraordinary events which occurred in the battle for the English Curriculum (Cox, 1995). There were more revisions to English than any other subject in the National Curriculum; the 'debate' about what should be included in the curriculum was driven by a right wing imperative to seize control from the academics and professional teachers of English; right wing politicians and writers from the government 'think tank' wanted to shift the agenda from a democratic, culturally inclusive agenda towards a nationalistic, 'Little England', élitist curriculum; political interference occurred at every level and meticulously prepared protestations from well known academics like Brian Cox and Professor Katharine Perera were ignored and dismissed (Cox, 1995); the orchestrated, 'new right' campaign to influence the curriculum was conducted in a high-handed and secretive manner; the National Literacy Strategy under a Labour Government was steamrollered into implementation in 1998 before teachers had a chance to benefit from the findings of the National Literacy Strategy Evaluation Project in 1997, in a determined attempt to drive up standards.

Compare the events of these turbulent times to what being an English teacher meant to Barnes (2000: 3) in the 1960s:

> What we were looking for was an English curriculum that recognised and strengthened all young people's ability through language to think and feel responsibly about the world they were living in, and we believed that literature had a major part to play in this. Far from regarding this policy as an abandonment of values, we were seeking a way of teaching English that would realise democratic and critical values within the confines of an education system that was far from *laissez faire*.

It is interesting to discover that Barnes, a major influence on those teachers who began their teaching career in the 1960s, continues to believe that these words are as relevant today as they were some forty years ago. Sticking to core beliefs such as those outlined above needs a gritty courage and steadfastness of conviction given the reductive and over-prescribed curriculum of the National Literacy Strategy. Yet, I would argue that teaching English with enthusiasm and commitment is, to some extent, dependent on firmly held beliefs about children, how they learn and the power of language to give children not only skills, pleasure, enjoyment, knowledge and understanding, but a means of helping them to make sense of their lives and a better chance of playing an active part in the democratic processes of the world in which they live.

Teachers striving for excellence are among those who have stuck to their beliefs and values regardless of how many obstacles stood in their way. It is this fact, among a host of others already mentioned, which fuelled their energy and kept their light burning.

Excellence

The political discourse of standards and achievement in English will usually include some or indeed all of the following terms and phrases: 'excellence', 'standards', 'targets', 'objectives', 'accountability', 'quality', 'fast-track experts', 'learning outcomes', 'booster classes', 'league tables', 'test scores' and so on. Some of these are straightforward; others are more elusive like 'quality', 'standards', 'excellence', 'good practice', for example. If these words are used often enough over time, they develop an association with political correctness which means that each time one or more of them is mentioned, the speaker or writer is assumed to be 'up to speed' and 'on message'. Despite the fact that such terms are rarely defined, they become the 'buzz words' of a new orthodoxy on teaching. Use them as many times as you like, do not worry about explaining their meaning and you will be judged to be 'in the know', and 'right on' as far as the latest literacy initiative is concerned. A week is a long time in the subject of English, so you need to be a quick reader and assimilator of knowledge if you wish to remain in the vanguard. Failure to use these terms can mean that you are perceived by others as out of touch, and in need of 'upskilling'! The problem is that after a while, the words are so over used that they become ubiquitous and eventually devoid of meaning.

This is one of the problems with the word 'excellence'. Everybody assumes that everyone who uses the term knows exactly what they mean and that it carries the same meaning for us all. Readers of this book will quickly discover that each of the authors has his or her own understanding of what excellence means and whilst there are discernible common strands, there is, as Silcock (2001: 2) pointed out, 'no single profile of excellent practice which will help us judge teaching [although] there are subject-specific profiles or models which have much in common'. The concept of 'excellence' is not therefore assumed to be straightforward. It is examined in these pages as a problematic and contested notion which will not readily yield up a recipe formula or handy hints for teachers. This does not mean the issue has been ducked or given over to yet another set of new questions. Excellence is not explored in a vacuum but in the specific context of the National Curriculum (DfEE/QCA, 2000) and the National Literacy Strategy Framework for Teaching (DfEE, 1998).

The key task of this book is to offer help to teachers, student teachers and teacher educators who are themselves grappling with what this term means in the context of teaching and classroom practice. Each of the authors has been asked to address themselves specifically to the question of excellence and how they believe they achieve it. What they have done is to make explicit what they do in the aspects of English they teach, outlining the materials and resources they use and how they use them.

While it is hoped that a great deal can be learned from the articulated experience of the writers in this book, a note of caution needs to be sounded. The difficulties to be surmounted in the achievement of excellence cannot be under-estimated. Given the proliferation of bureaucratic demands in a target-laden and standards-driven culture, finding the energy to address these requirements as well as achieve the highest possible levels of teaching, is a Herculean endeavour. What this book does not set out to do is to set a gold standard for excellence which only the strongest and most able teachers can achieve. This would be tantamount to condoning an élitist culture of English teaching. It is simply not possible for the majority or even the minority of teachers to achieve excellence in every lesson they teach; this would be too high a price to pay in terms of emotional, mental and physical health. Stress and burn-out among hard working teachers are already acknowledged problems within the profession and we would not wish to add yet a further set of demands for teachers to have to respond to either implicitly or ex-plicitly. The real task is to find ways of making the achievement of excellence more widely accessible. How can this be done? Whilst the National Literacy Strategy Framework for Teaching is in the opinion of many practitioners over structured and cumbersome in its prescriptions, the process of making it work for teachers and children since its implementation in 1998, has produced some excellent training materials (*c.f.* DfEE, 2000; 2001), teaching guidance and resource packs. Seldom have teachers had better access to well written resources and training courses. However, the focus has concentrated almost exclusively on literacy with the result that speaking and listening or oracy, as it was called in the 1960s, is in danger of being squeezed out. This was a fertile time for classroom innovation and the pioneering work which was done by Barnes *et al.* (1969) on the relationship between talk and learning was a significant moment in the history of English teaching. Drawing on the work of Vygotsky (1962) these writers showed the extent to which pupils' writing improved when they were allowed to express their thoughts aloud to groups of children and interested adults. Vygotsky believed that if speech in childhood lays the foundation for a lifetime of thinking, teachers had a central role to play in scaffolding children's developing ability to clarify, shape and organise what they wanted to say and write. The work of Barnes *et al.* was subsequently taken up and developed by Wells (1987) and more recently by the National Oracy Project (Barnes and Sheeran, 1992). For the first time since the Bullock Report (1975) teachers have access to some first rate materials, resources and guidance for organising and constructing an oracy curriculum. Now that reading and writing is in the ascendancy, oracy has assumed a less important place in the English curriculum. If the lessons which teachers have learned about the positive impact which talk can have on learning in general, and reading and writing in particular, could now be harnessed to the teaching and learning of literacy, teachers would have a powerful set of pedagogical tools from which they could develop the potential for excellence.

Giving children greater opportunities for talk through drama, discussion, prepared presentations and the like would also accord more closely with teachers' beliefs about how children best learn.

Several of the writers in this book stress the importance of the place which talk occupies in understanding new concepts, reaching for deeper meanings in literature, in learning how language works in different genres and in learning to use another language, for example. What is also important to remember in all the talk about excellence, target-setting, increased test scores and so on, is that language is at the core of what makes us human. We need to find imaginative and creative ways to integrate more explicitly the crucial relationship between speaking and listening, reading and writing so that what children are required to do is worthwhile on their terms, not because they have to meet a certain objective at a specified time in the year.

A further potential for excellence exists in relation to what teachers now know about how language works with respect to grammar and genre approaches to literacy. If this knowledge could be taught to children as a form of metalanguage, they would then have the necessary language, knowledge and authority to help each other improve their writing and understanding about differing literary forms (see Brundrett *et al.*, 2001). This is an area which is ripe for research and investigation. For now, the combination of a renewed commitment to oral language with pedagogical strategies designed to help children acquire a metalanguage for analysing their own writing could become a powerful synergy for change along with a new direction for excellence.

1. Shakespeare, Excellence and the Young Writer

Fred Sedgwick

'The brightness of his eye gives life to the sun ...'
'The tartness of his face sours ripe grapes ...'
'The march of his gait is terror to the small ...'
'Her sharpness makes sure of emptiness and hate ...'

What is excellence? Many accounts and many analyses of teaching begin with a definition or, even more tiresomely, a series of definitions. The dictionary says this, the dictionary says that. Defining terms feels necessary to the writer (if less so to the reader) because this preliminary activity is often, merely, a matter of nearly, but not quite, getting started, of getting the feet wet, of delaying the arrival of the real matter, when serious thinking has to be done. It is the warm-up to the match, while the crowd is waiting for the real thing to begin.

The truly desperate writer (I have been that man, all too many times) will resort, shamelessly, to the *Thesaurus* and the spurious creativity that lists of synonyms can suggest. To open with definitions is something of a cliché, and therefore I do not want to begin in that way here.

Nevertheless, educators need to understand what they mean by the word 'excellence'; not in a dictionary or thesaurus sense, which both imply objectivity, but in another sense that I want to explore in this introduction. What is excellent, first, for you and me; and second for that other person lurking purposefully at the back of our classrooms – inspector, perhaps, or student, or headteacher – at least in terms of the title of this chapter?

No doubt other writers in this book have addressed this question in terms of their titles. I will attempt an answer in terms of mine: Shakespeare, children and their writing. With the necessary changes, it applies to my other chapter on teaching poetry as well.

Most educators take excellence for granted, much as they take for granted the apparently benign (but deeply duplicitous) phrase 'good practice'. They talk about excellence as though they all mean exactly the same thing by the word, as though it was like 'road' or 'cat' or 'lamp-post', begging no troubled reflections, no debate, no disagreements. We know (or think we know) about roads and cats and lamp posts. Excellence is, on the contrary, a subjective and complex matter. I think roads, cats and lamp-posts are, too, but that is another story.

To say what we think is excellent (as well as to say what we think is 'good practice') is to give away our ideological position. To put it bluntly, it is to own up to what we think human beings, especially children, are; it is to give away our politics, our ethics and sometimes, even, our religion. To try to show what I mean, I shall take an example from politics: is an excellent society one in which there is a virtual certainty of order? Or is it one in which there is total freedom to speak as we want? The politics of the first kind of society would be conserving of established values. It is not difficult to think of examples of things that leaders in such a society would want to preserve. Monarchy, an established church, a hereditary chamber in parliament, a privileged system of education that benefits the upper and middle classes at the expense of the rest – these will serve as a few examples. Such a society would be concerned with clichés, because clichés are about understanding, writing about and thereby preserving what we already know. It would be about (to use a cliché) not rocking the boat. It would be right-wing. It would look like:

> The heavens themselves, the planets, and this centre
> [that] observe degree, priority, and place ...
> Office, and custom, in all line of order ...
> (Ulysses, in *Troilus and Cressida*)

The politics of the second would be in contrast. They would be about challenging what has been accepted; about making phrases that are not clichés. Two of the things in society that leaders would want to clear away would be inequality of opportunity in health and education. Leaders of such a society would claim that they would be happy with the risks involved in allowing free speech in all settings, including, dare I write it, classrooms. It would, of course, be left-wing. (This is not to deny that most left-wing societies so far have suppressed free speech eventually, but that is another story). Ulysses described such a society (from his conservative perspective – not, need I say, Shakespeare's) as one where

> ... the planets
> In evil mixture to disorder wander,
> What plagues, and what portents, what mutiny,
> What raging of the sea, shaking of earth,
> Commotion in the winds, frights, changes, horrors,
> Divert and crack, rend and deracinate
> The unity and married calm of states
> Quite from their fixture!

I see these two sets of politics clearly as I write on the day after Mayday 2000. The first set is there in the newspapers' outraged reaction (resembling Ulysses' prophesies above, but without their eloquence) to what the anti-capitalist demonstrators did to Sir Winston Churchill's statue, daubing red and green paint over it and giving it an absurd green Mohican hairdo. The second is there, of course, in those very actions.

This is necessarily a statement and illustration of extreme positions. In fact, of course, we are dealing with a continuum on which there are an infinite number of points. That does not invalidate my last paragraph. I just want, at the moment, to set out the terms for any debate; to put a framework down in which the reader may, if he or she chooses, place the examples of teaching and learning that I give later on. I recognise that at different times and on different issues, we all find ourselves at different places on that continuum. I recognise, for example, that order, many established values and even clichés are necessary. I require 'brotherhoods in cities, /Peaceful commerce from dividable shores' (Ulysses again).

Barthes and Sontag (1982) wrote about the order/autonomy debate with great elegance, about the safe edge and the cutting edge:

> Two edges are created: an obedient, conformist, plagiarising edge (the language is to be copied in its canonical state, as it has been established by schooling, good usage, culture), and another edge, mobile, blank, (ready to assume any contours), which is never anything but the site of its effect: the place where the death of language is glimpsed.

This wonderful passage suggests to us two things: one is that we cannot live without the cliché, the blunt edge. We have to be obedient. Life would be impossible otherwise. Think of driving on the wrong side of the road, or of neglecting for any length of time to pay our tax return, or of neglecting the mess our dogs make. Think of running constantly against the grain of what I will call 'common sense' (more of which later). But we will be uncreative, uneducated (and poor educators, more to the point) if are not alert to the moving edge, which is always on the point of risk; where the 'death of language' (as Barthes terrifyingly puts it) is always to be glimpsed; where the teacher might be exposed as ignorant, and where the pupil will teach him or her something; where 'degree in schools' (Ulysses again) might be compromised. We will fail to teach, we will merely school or train, if we are to accept, unquestioningly, the accepted tabloid stance on anything.

To come back, explicitly, to education: to some, excellence in the English curriculum is about raising standards, which seems to do with the numbers of children who pass tests; who will be able to answer questions correctly, about English generally, and about Shakespeare's plays in particular. I will gladly give away my politics and my ethics here: to call this 'raising standards' is a perversion of language. It is taking an obsession with order to the point where statistics and headlines matter more than human beings and learning. To use a Marxist term, it is to reify statistics. It is a false consciousness. I will give away my religion, too: as every human being was born in the image of God, to treat him or her as a statistic is a blasphemy.

Not everyone is so frank. People who believe in excellence as part of test results hold a political position, but it is hidden as far as they can keep it hidden. That position is about control. They pretend to objectivity.

My themes, then, are control (let the plagiarising edge cut through what it will) and autonomy (dare we acknowledge in our thinking, writing and teaching the mobile blankness that risks exposing our pedagogical inadequacy and the intellectual and emotional acuity of our students; that risks even the death of language?). The control is control of the children and the teacher (and all adults involved with children in schools). The autonomy (in contrast) is autonomy for them to be brave, to take risks. Implicit in this chapter is the idea that the great task after the new millennium is not, except in the short term, how to implement policies and practices imposed on workers in schools as mere hired hands (as the literacy strategy and other ring-bound files would have us believe); not, that is, merely to obey the orders of those who are confident about the objective existence of 'good practice' (when all that notion contains is a notion of what the powerful have decided is good, a very different notion); but how to stay human and autonomous in the face of these policies, that practice, all these ring-bound files and all the statutory require-ments that come with them.

In other words, this chapter is about how to retain the essential creativity of teaching and learning Shakespeare in the face of a mechanistic assault that has great power, not least because of its taken-for-granted nature, its accepted but not questioned politics, but also because of a connected reason: its hegemony over the past twenty years. The machine has managerialised the work of teachers, making them hired hands rather than semi-autonomous and potentially creative educators. Together, teachers have to talk, and discuss, and write, and collaborate in an attempt to reclaim schools for their children and themselves.

Interlude

What about the four lines at the beginning of my chapter? What do you think of them? Are they any good? One, of course, is Shakespeare's. The others are by 10-year-old children.

Is any of the four excellent? Or are all of them? Which is most excellent? Once you have decided which, decide why you think that:

Is one of the lines poor?
And what play is the Shakespeare line from?

So you know. Well done. And if you do not:

If Shakespeare is so excellent, why do you not know?

No, I am not being more knowledgeable than thou. I would not have known which was the Shakespeare line until a few weeks ago. I found it, reading the play it comes from for the second time – I had heard it on radio, but had never seen it on television or stage – and thought: that line is good. My thinking then went something like this: There is something acid about it – it is a fragment of life as I know it – could be a description of a flinty face – it is a piece of Shakespeare that children would understand – it would not put them off – the structure of the line is all-important – if we can help the children to keep that structure, while varying all the line's components, they will write a good line themselves, and learn something about Shakespeare's method.

This way of dealing with a single line (which I have discussed in my book on teaching Shakespeare (1999: 20) – where the line is 'He wears the rose of youth upon him' from *Antony and Cleopatra*) is like the old folk story of the woodsman's axe. The blade gets blunt, and he sharpens it, many times. Eventually, he throws the blade away, and replaces it. The handle becomes worn, and he throws that away and replaces that. This process happens, say, twenty times in his working life. He dies and the axe is passed on to his son. But is it the same axe? Yes and no. Similarly, the children will discard all the components in Shakespeare's line, and replace them with other components – still retaining the same structure. The analogy breaks down. All analogies break down eventually. The line, of course, is no longer Shakespeare's, but it does have the same structure.

My thought process continued: I have got to teach it! In fact, I could not wait to get into a school and meet some juniors to try the idea out. **End of interlude**

How does Shakespeare fit into the ideological framework I was trying to build before that interlude? It ought to be said right away that to claim him as a conservative on the strength of the Ulysses speech that I have quoted from would be a mistake: that is a character speaking (not a very pleasant character), not the writer. I am not concerned with Shakespeare's politics, but with what 'excellent' means in terms of teaching him. I am going back to the beginning.

Excellence has often been assumed to be about these three things. First, teaching Shakespeare as a historical element in a nationalistic teaching of England. Laurence Olivier's film of *Henry V* exemplifies this approach. It has great value to those who see education as essentially a means of preserving an established order, and who value the notion of the greatness of Britain; who see Shakespeare's plays and poems as emblems of a hierarchy that includes, well, the Book of Common Prayer, the Royal Family, and 'spinsters cycling to Evensong' and 'warm beer in country pubs' (to borrow John Major's formulation of Englishness). This teaching suits those with Ulysses' perspective, but is of no use to those concerned with the language and the learning about it. It is essentially sentimental in it that depicts the Tudor world as a Merrie England where the poor did not exist (unlike, of course, in Shakespeare's plays); that depicts Shakespeare, the writer and the man, as interesting largely in terms of the history of his times; that reduces the plays essentially to beautiful pictures of women in flounces and men in tights and codpieces, speaking English verse in RP (received pronunciation) accents unlike (we can be sure) the Midland accent that Shakespeare spoke in.

Excellence has often been assumed to be a production of a play by Shakespeare which has been re-written by one or more of the teachers. Putting on 'simplified' versions of the plays written by 'Sir' or 'Miss' may seem like common sense – but is nothing to do with education. It is more to do with display: display, not of what children can do, or have done, or will do, but of the skills of 'Sir' or 'Miss'; it is to do with display of the costumes made by an army of parents, display of the school as part of that display project that every school has to undertake in these days: public relations, to put it bluntly, not education; selling glossy surfaces to unsuspecting parents, while neglecting the realties that are often squalid.

My view is that excellence in the teaching of Shakespeare will be teaching that helps children to focus on nothing but the following two elements: the language of the text, and learning about it. That is – the autonomy of the language, and the autonomy of the learner. As I have written before (1999), we do not need to study whole plays. Concentrating on one scene, one speech, one word even helps the teacher and the learner to see how Shakespeare uses the language. I was pleased to see in *The Observer* (Arnold, 2000) that this approach has other uses. The radio critic recorded how the director Fiona Shaw:

> asked the actors to pick what they thought were the three salient phrases from the post-Duncan murder scene in *Macbeth* and repeat them. After that she got them to whittle them down to one phrase, one word, and then one syllable.

Such an approach startles us – teachers, children, actors, readers – for two reasons. First, we are used to thinking of Shakespeare as huge. He is, at worst, perceived as an unapproachable Leviathan: however much we study his works, he will always evade us. At best, he is 'myriad-minded Shakespeare' (Coleridge). This exercise helps us to see him as gem-like: small, strong and beautiful. Second, this process startles us by focusing closely, as through a microscope, on Shakespeare's use of language. To get an idea, teachers might like to look at Vendler's (1997) amazing edition of Shakespeare's *Sonnets*, where she eschews any biographical speculation about the characters in the poems – poet, young man, dark lady, rival poet – in favour of taking King Lear's advice to 'look with thine ears'; using her ears as intently as she can in order to get to the heart of the language of these poems; and hence – there is no other way – to the heart of the poems themselves.

Here is another example of this approach, using a line I have already quoted. In *Coriolanus*, Act 5 Scene 4, Menenius describes Coriolanus:

> The tartness of his face sours ripe grapes; when he walks, he moves like an engine, and the ground shrinks before his treading. He is able to pierce a corslet with his eye …

Take no more than the first sentence of this passage. The sharp sounds of the letters 't' and 'p' (sounds that hardly require much opening of the mouth) and the hissing of the letter 's' repeated, as well as the sound of the 'c' in 'face', all contribute powerfully to the picture of implacability that Menenius is drawing here. The way to convey this to young writers is to say the line emphasising these sounds and the mood of sourness, and to get them to do the same. Then go in closer: play with the keywords in the line, 'tart', 'face', 'sour' and 'grapes', speaking them more and more intensely, trying to convey their meaning. Ask the children which syllable most dramatically expresses the mood of the line. Finally, point out to the children the exaggeration (technically 'hyperbole') of the image of the powerful, bitter man who is, appallingly, capable of souring 'ripe grapes'. There are some examples of children writing after this exercise on page 20.

Interlude: is Shakespeare the greatest?

Bloom (1998) claimed that we were not, until Shakespeare wrote his plays and poems, truly human. Bloom's book is rare amongst literary criticism in its readability. It is elegant, opinionated, full of little insights and surprises, and, though I think it is often wrong-headed – on Shylock, for example, for Bloom a 'comic villain' – I would not want to be without my copy for very long. But this kind of exaggeration is absurd, and leads me to another point about excellence. It is counter-productive to tell children in any terms about Shakespeare's excellence or, worse, greatness, even in terms less overblown than Bloom's deification. I agree with the American poet John Berryman, quoted by James Wood in *The Guardian* for the 6th of May, 2000, when he said that to be constantly 'credulous' before Shakespeare is to be naïve. To assume that every line he wrote was great is to turn him into stone. 'Shakespeare was a writer, fallible like any other' Wood commented. Samuel Johnson wrote that 'Shakespeare never had six lines together without a fault. Perhaps you may find seven …'.

It is important to be critical of Shakespeare as we are about any other writer. There is another reason for this, which is to do with the young writers we are teaching. I was making this point to a fellow teacher of English and she replied 'Why? He is great, isn't he?' But consider: a student is told that Shakespeare is 'great' and then comes across these lines from *Hamlet*:

> Full thirty times hath Phoebus' cart gone round
> Neptune's salt wash and Tellus' orbed ground,
> And thirty dozen moons with borrowed sheen
> About the world have twelve times twelve thirties been
> Since love our hands and Hymen did our hearts
> Unite ...

Once it has been explained that this 'trudging verse' (Sutherland and Watts, 2000) is (however the metre trudges) imagistically, deliberately over-wrought; that Phoebus is the sun, Neptune the god of the sea, Tellus the earth; that thirty dozen moons means 360 months; and that Hymen is the goddess of marriage ... once all this has been explained, nothing will repair the damage caused by the juxta-position of two supposed facts: Shakespeare is great, and this language is turgid and dull.

Or again, the student may read or hear the opening lines of *Measure for Measure*. I re-read the Duke's speech, from 'Of government' to 'we remember' every few months, hoping, in vain, to find it clearer; comforted only by the possible fact that its obscurity is deliberate on Shakespeare's part, telling us something about the obfuscating nature of this politician. The contrast between the opacity of these lines and the clarity of Escalus' three lines that follow them bears out this theory.

Again, imagine young readers coming across those lines with the 'Shakespeare is the greatest' *mantra* ringing in their ears. I think of a cartoon I saw years ago: two teenagers are listening to a Beethoven symphony on their little Dansette record-player (that dates my story somewhere in the late 1960s or early 1970s). One is saying to the other, with a puzzled and disappointed expression: 'I don't feel anything yet, do you?' The expectations had been something along these lines: Beethoven is great, they all say so, parents and teachers especially; I am not feeling any magic now; I must be an also-ran, or even a non-starter, in the Beethoven appreciation stakes.

It is all too easy to see the same process happening with Shakespeare, unless we as teachers take our responsibilities carefully, and avoid the easy commonsensical 'Shakespeare is the greatest' line, and instead find entry points for young readers and writers, while also demystifying Shakespeare (it is not difficult, and indeed, this is the principle subject of this chapter); scraping away the barnacles of casual usage, 'Bard', 'Swan of Avon', England's greatest glory and so on, and on, and on. If I have a project, here and earlier (Sedgwick, 1999), it is to 'de-Bardolize', 'unSwan' Shakespeare. This has to be done before we can help young writers to make Shakespeare even remotely theirs.

Shakespeare can be dull to us, because our ears are not attuned to his often long and complicated sentences, his journeying syntax, his habit of piling metaphor on metaphor. His contemporaries were simply better listeners than we are. To pretend that we will appreciate glory in every word we read is silly, and damaging to the young readers coming to Shakespeare's plays for the first time. It is true (as Iain Sinclair said on Radio 3) that Shakespeare's:

> elusiveness is absolute. He succeeds, more than any other English poet, in doing the thing that all writers aspire to: he vanishes, completely, into his own language; and through his disappearance, he leaves us with those mysterious engines, the plays, which remain powerful enough to resist any perverse interpretation. (Quoted by Lezard, 2000)

One implication of these remarks by Sinclair is that Shakespeare can resist other perversions, as well as bad productions of his plays. He will survive narcissistic teachers seeing themselves as writers and directors of productions of the plays, with the pupils running obediently around as a Titania and Bottom, 'de-Shakespeared' and dis-empowered, and further fouled by being 'Sirred' or 'Missed'. He has survived the barren historical approach, and all the 'bardolizing' of tourists, princes of Wales, and editorial writers in newspapers. He will survive his damaging status as national poet. He will survive, whatever mistakes we may make when we teach him in what I think is (in contrast to all the above) the educational way: by concentrating on his words, and the learning that has to be done to understand, interpret and enjoy them. And by accepting that, as teachers, we must be learners too: taught by Shakespeare, and taught, as well, by our students, who will, given the opportunity – the autonomy – come up with insights from their fresh perspectives that are beyond us.
End of interlude

Children writing

The tartness of his face sours ripe grapes.

The brightness of his eye gives life to the sun.

The fire of her heart burns grass away.

The sharpness in her pupils picks holes in them.

The ice of their brains chills my intelligence.

The softness of his head squidges against my legs.
(The line above was brought about by a baby crawling on the carpet as the rest of the family played a card game; the writer had felt her brother's head pushing at her calves.)

The greatness of his belly nudges them.
(An unintentional depiction of Falstaff in the Boar's Head tavern!)

The sweetness of her thinking rots my teeth.

As I often do, I sent my friend Sophie Chipperfield this idea, and her pupils (they are 9 and 10 years old) came up with the following:

The evil of her lips gives poison to an apple. (Charlotte)

The ugliness of her frown turns day into night.
The fury in his finger could spin the world out of space. (Adam)

The stench of my breath could scare away death.
The evil in his brain could outwit the world. (Matthew)

The coldness of his stare freezes volcano lava. (Ruth)

The heaviness of his eyes is enough to flatten crystal.
The alertness of his face makes security cameras look asleep. (Ruth C)

The darkness of his heart makes the sky turn black. (Hannah)

Charlotte's line reminded me of the story of *Snow White*. The line is a variation on the theme of apples and poison. It is a reversal of the familiar fairy story plot which might, in part, be summed up 'the evil of the apple gives poison to the girl'. Perhaps the evil step-mother turns up again in Adam's first sentence. This theme in turn is a variation of the story of the fall of Adam and Eve in the Garden of Eden.

When children write, they never come to their notebooks or word processors with only what the teacher has said: in this case, what the teacher has said about Shakespeare. Unconsciously, subconsciously or consciously, they bring with them into the classroom many experiences and, as in this case, many stories. They bring potent symbols and myths to bear on their writing. This is a way of saying that they are active, not passive learners.

In this, of course, they are like Shakespeare. His plots came from all over his contemporary culture and fomented in his active mind. Anyone who thinks that his plots are central to his achievement (as opposed to what he did with his plots) should reflect on the fact that, for example, *Twelfth Night* 'is based mainly on the tale of Apollonius and Silla in Barnabe Riche's *Farewell to the Military Profession* (1581)'. See Wells (1978) for an account of where Shakespeare found his stories, his myths.

Some of the myths the children bring (darkness and light haunt many of these lines, much as they haunt the early chapters of Genesis, even though they are not present in the line from *Coriolanus* that started this lesson) are as old as the first story teller. Others, like the security camera, are new.

I have written several times before about how, if we pay attention to children's writing, we will learn about them, their learning and our teaching. Look at these pieces. How well the children write. Look at the movement, helped by the alliteration in, for example, 'The fury in his finger could spin the world out of space'. The sentence 'The stench of my breath could scare away death' shows an intuitive grasp of both assonance (the vowel sounds in all the main words) and alliteration, as well as a suitable sense of melodrama (see *Titus Andronicus*). How well the children write, indeed, with the teaching of a teacher who (resisting the pressure to be a hired hand meekly delivering the current government's requirements) cares about what they write. How well the children write with the ghostly presence of Shakespeare. How much better they would write, had they the chance to re-draft their work. That was impossible given the request I had made to Sophie; it was probably impossible for Shakespeare, given other, more demanding pressures.

One entry point from *As You Like It*

One of the easiest entry points comes in Act 2 Scene 7 of *As You Like It*. I have written about teaching this speech before (Sedgwick, 1999: 73) but in this chapter I take the work a little further. I had just heard an excellent production of this play on the radio, but was struck as usual how the actor playing Jaques always finds it impossible to come into the conversation with the famous lines beginning 'All's the world's a stage …' with anything like a natural approach. I performed these lines – 'hammed them up', I suppose – to a group of middle school children on a course for young writers.

> All the world's a stage,
> And all the men and women merely players.
> They have their exits and their entrances;
> And one man in his time plays many parts,
> His acts being ages seven. At first the infant,
> Mewling and puking in the nurse's arms;
> Then the whining schoolboy, with his satchel
> And shining morning face, creeping like snail
> Unwillingly to school. And then the lover,
> Sighing like furnace, with a woeful ballad
> Made to his mistress' eyebrow. Then a soldier,
> Full of strange oaths, and bearded like the pard,
> Jealous in honour, sudden and quick in quarrel,
> Seeking the bubble reputation
> Even in the cannon's mouth. And then the justice,
> In fair round belly with good capon lin'd,
> With eyes severe and beard of formal cut,
> Full of wise saws and modern instances;
> And so he plays his part. The sixth age shifts
> Into the lean and slippered pantaloon,
> With spectacles on nose and pouch on side,
> His youthful hose, well sav'd, a world too wide
> For his shrunk shank; and his big manly voice,
> Turning again towards childish treble, pipes
> And whistles in his sound. Last scene of all,
> That ends this strange eventful history,
> Is second childishness and mere oblivion;
> Sans teeth, sans eyes, sans taste, sans everything.

I explained some difficult terms, such as 'pard' (leopard), 'woeful ballad /Made to his mistress' eyebrow', and 'sans', and then we performed the speech together, muling and puking early on, whining with an aged treble at the end, and with a full gamut of vocal sounds in between: sentimental lover, marching soldier (note how his lines, from 'Full of strange oaths, and bearded like the pard ...' onwards enact a march) and pompous justice. I then asked the children to write their own version: not of the whole speech, but of a chosen section. Certain parts of the speech – the schoolchild and the old man – appealed to the writers more than the others:

> The baby crying, weeping for its rattle, pink and blue,
> whanging for a drop of warm milk ready from the microwave,
> but then, when night falls, peace, quiet, until ...

> The schoolchild mopes mournfully to school
> scuffing hated school shoes in despair
> turning up the road to imprisonment.

> The schoolchild, quiet when he wants to be
> and loud and noisy when he doesn't
> dawdling to school as though he has all the time in the world
> and making silly excuses when confronted ...

> The schoolgirl being forced to enter lessons
> answering reluctantly the register,
> secretly rolling up her skirt
> being shouted out: 'Skirt on the knee!'

> The lovers, committed, connected on their wedding day
> flirting along all night, all day,
> growing too old, but will they stay
> forever, forever, till death do us part?

> The businessman, smartly dressed and ready for a day's work,
> His schedule neatly typed, his meetings listed,
> His desk neat, all his equipment organised.

> The door to door salesman dragging his display case,
> his crafty smile and pleasant convincing tone

as he flogs off his goods to his unsuspecting victims.

The landlord of a pub calling for last orders again,
yelling, *go away it's closing time at last!*,
pushing the grumbling drunks out of the door.

The old wrinkled man with low voice breaks back to infant's voice.

The old man, bedridden and dreaming
about his younger days sighs his last breath ...

The old man sits in his dressing gown
watching UK Gold replays.

The modern diction: 'microwave ... UK Gold replays ... Skirt on the knee! ... schedule neatly typed, his meetings listed' helps to demystify Shakespeare for these young people. It helps to 'de-Bardify', to 'un-Swan' Shakespeare's words. This in turn is likely to help them to make Shakespeare's theirs, rather that the possession of some powerful group. It enables them to link the words of Jaques with their own; to see a bridge between Shakespeare and themselves that 'Bardolatry' and 'Swanning' will never build.

I note here that this exercise has enabled the children to refer to their own lives and their tribulations: discipline in school, for example; and to anticipate problems in the future. Much good creative writing is a kind of rehearsal for life, and here the lines about the young lovers seem especially poignant. Writers using this passage seem to be reflecting wryly on their own memories and current lives. They also reflect on their futures.

An entry point from *King Lear* (Act 3 Scene 2)

Poor Tom; that eats the swimming frog; the toad, the tadpole, the wall-newt, and the water; that in the fury of his heart, when the foul fiend rages, eats cow-dung for salads, swallows the old rat and the ditch-dog; drinks the green mantle of the standing pool; who is whipped from tithing to tithing, and stock-punished, and imprisoned; who hath three suits to his back, six shirts to his body:

Horse to ride, and weapon to wear;
But mice and rats and such small deer

Have been Tom's food for seven long year.
Beware my follower. Peace, Smulkin! peace, thou fiend.

I wrote my version, quickly, in a notebook that I carry everywhere, while the children were finishing another task. This was partly to demonstrate that you do not have to be Shakespeare or a child in school to write, or have to write. This is a useful lesson to teach as often as possible in this practical way, because, by our normal practice, students learn implicitly that only great artists and prisoners in schools write, or have to write. Also, my writing (thin and extremely derivative as it is) provided a useful 'de-Bardifying', 'un-Swanning' bridge between the Shakespeare passage and the children's work:

> Poor man, that drinks discarded ale from tankards in pub gardens; that greets girls with blown kisses, boys with wavings of his wet fists; who burrows like a rat in waste bins, searching for butts of cigarettes; who is chased from the gardens with the curses and cries of the privileged sane sailing behind him; who, in his innocent lunacy, splashes, smacking the water of the village duckpond, raucously and rancorously denouncing the rancid deacons of the local church ... Poor man, that once sat in pews, in a jury box, on a hill gazing down at the Gloucestershire hills ... Have a kind of peace, thinks this passer-by, dropping palm-warm pence into your hat. Have a kind of peace, and a fresh cigarette, and a half of some golden ale.

Oxymorons

An oxymoron is

> a figure of speech in which contradictory terms are brought together in what is at first sight an impossible combination ... [examples are] 'I burn and freeze like ice [and] the darkness visible of Hell in Milton's *Paradise Lost*'. (Gray, 1984)

There are oxymorons of a kind in *Timon of Athens* (Act 4 Scene 3):

> Thus much of this will make black white, foul fair,
> Wrong right, base noble, old young, coward valiant ...

Gibson, in his edition of *Romeo and Juliet* for schools, pointed out that 'much of [that] play is about the clash of opposites' and that therefore 'oxymorons are particularly appropriate ...'. It is probably enough to give a few examples here (but see Sedgwick, 1999 for list of Romeo's and Juliet's oxymorons):

> brawling love, loving hate, heavy lightness, feather of lead, bright smoke, cold fire, sick health, beautiful tyrant, fiend angelical, damned saint, honourable villain.

I ask young writers to identify what is going on in those lines. Somebody noticed that each line was made up of 'opposites'. I took this further, and introduced the technical word. The children then simply listed all the oxymorons that they could think off, and then chose their favourites and made them into little 'oxymoronic poems':

> Black light
> that
> brightly fades
> with creative destruction
> and destructive peace.
>
> Silent thunder
> that
> strikes quietly.
>
> Flying submarine
> that
> slowly speeds
> over
> black snow
> in the white night.

Insults

Shakespeare's Insults by Hill and Ottchen (1991) was a liberating discovery in my teaching of Shakespeare. I have written about it and its influence in my own 1999 book. Here I want to take this technique one stage further, using a passage from *Henry IV Part One*.

Early in this play, the young Prince Hal 'consorts' (as we say) with the drunken lowlife of Eastcheap: Ned Poins, Bardolph, the Hostess, Peto and, most importantly, the cowardly, greedy and yet infinitely witty fat old man Sir John Falstaff (who, for many, myself included, is Shakespeare's greatest creation). In this scene, the Prince is playing a game with Falstaff. The Prince is pretending to be his father the King, while Falstaff is acting the part of the Prince. These words are, then, the King's words to the Prince as imagined by the Prince:

> There is a devil haunts thee in the likeness of an old fat man, a tun of man is thy companion. Why dost thou converse with that trunk of humours, that bolting-hatch of beastliness, that swollen parcel of dropsies, that huge bombard of sack, that stuffed cloak-bag of guts, that roasted Manningtree ox with the pudding in his belly, that reverend Vice, that grey Iniquity, that Father Ruffian, that Vanity in years? Wherein is he good, but to taste sack and drink it? Wherein cunning, but in craft? Wherein crafty, but in villainy? Wherein villainous, but in all things? Wherein worthy, but in nothing? (Act 2 Scene 4)

The now-read-on that I have given above is not necessary for children to appreciate what this speech is: a gloriously robust catalogue of insults for a fat man. Children love playing with it, speaking alternative sections, for example, to be unpleasant to each other. I ask them to pick out the most vivid 'fat' words, and typically they offer these: 'tun', 'trunk', 'swollen', 'stuffed', 'ox' and 'belly'. It takes very little teaching (though a little radio-acting, perhaps) to pull out the other words that are something to do with fatness: 'bolting-hatch' (waste-bin), 'parcel', 'bombard' (leather wine bottle), 'cloak-bag' and 'pudding'. I ask the children to note the repetitions near the end: 'Wherein is …?'. Then I suggest that they write insults for another person, a smoker, a drunk, a greedy person, a mean one, a giggler and so on.

You smoke, you choke,
you cough, you laugh,
you are a smoker but
never a joker.
You smell, you yell,
go to hell!,
for what you are,
stinky smoker,
your fags, your packs,
they smell, oh God,

I hate it now,
why don't you stop?,
your yellow teeth,
your lungs of tar.
I hate it, so
goodbye for now.

You are mad in your ways. Why do you meet that boulder of fat, that is only good for blocking drains and tunnels? He could put the lard business into bankruptcy. His weight would smash the elephant scales. The Russians want him for an anti-tank weapon. When he has a shower, even Australia issues a flood warning. Liposuction would take him a month. He gets his curries in articulated lorry containers. When he tripped over the Grand Canyon was formed. He is the eighth wonder of the world.

Sophie Chipperfield sent me some writing that had been done following study of the lines 'You shall not go till I set you up a glass /Where you may see the inmost part of you' (*Hamlet*, Act 3 Scene 4):

The glass would reveal
a girl sitting at a computer
transfixed by the world wide web,
a sea with dark blues and bright yellows in it.

The glass would reveal
the darkest storm cloud
but then it is washed away by the biggest brightest sun.

The glass would reveal
a crowd of people talking
about the lonely girl,
lonely just because she is different.

The glass would reveal
a horse running around a tiny paddock
and then the gate being opened and the horse is free.

The glass would reveal
a giraffe, tall and solitary.

There is in me
a worn-out girl running in a race
at the front, with an aggressive look on her face ...

a prison of words
full to the brim with things to say
never knowing where to start.

There is in me
a mainsail being hauled up the mast
powering the tiny dot ...
a snowflake being ski-ed on
by a thousand on the biggest mountain you've ever seen ...
a spelling book
with nothing written down ...
a candle growing instead of shrinking.

Conclusion: Shakespeare, young writers and common sense

The approaches to teaching Shakespeare I described at the beginning of this chapter – historical ones involving emphasising, though not showing, the greatness of 'The Bard', and involving, too, simplified versions of his plays written by teachers – might be described as common sense ones. They are rather like one of her Majesty's Inspector's saying (as he reportedly did the other day) that there is no point in young children listening to classical music in schools unless they had studied the historical background to that music. This sounds all right, but it is not. Children will get into the beginnings of appreciating music by listening to it, not by listening to talk about it.

Most common sense is deceptive in this way. It looks all right, but lets us down. It was common sense to put failing children in a corner with a dunce cap on, or to put them in prison for stealing bread. It was once common sense, not so long ago (and this deceptive idiocy is coming back) to arrange children in classes in terms of their supposed intelligence. We know these actions are wrong now.

Berowne and the King of Navarre (in *Love's Labour's Lost*) know the limitations of common sense:

Berowne: What is the end of study, let me know?
King: Why, that to know which else we would not know.
Berowne: Things hid and barr'd, you mean, from common sense?
King: Ay, that is study's godlike recompense …

Study's recompense in learning Shakespeare will transcend common sense, and lead young people into understanding about themselves and their world; understanding that we, as their teachers, can only guess at.

This poem was written by a 10-year-old boy after he had played with the speech 'I'll follow you' from *A Midsummer Night's Dream*, Act 3 Scene 1 (see Sedgwick, 1999 for more on this).

I'll follow you
through the A's and B's
where antelopes accompany bears.
I'll follow you
up and around Cs and Ds
dancing and drifting around cloakrooms.
I'll follow you
Under economy and over faucets and fax machines
then collect geese and gloves and grates.
I'll follow you,
where hammers and hamburgers hastily chase you,
to where infants invent
ingenious illusions
next to J
where juggernauts journey to Jersey
where kings and kitchens are in K.
Life and lifts light up L
and money menaces M
and naughty gnomes knock on N.
I'll follow you
over octopuses, olives and oxen.
Ps and Qs
practise pranks in the quiet queen's chambers.
R and S follow

for spiders' races in Supercross speedway.
Tarantulas terrorise tourists in tea that comes from Turkey.
I'll follow you
past unities and umbrellas in U
and violins vigorously playing a Viking tune.
We wish we could weave well from W
and see X-rays and xylophones in X.
I'll follow you
through Y and Z
zigzagging through zones of life.
I will follow you –
from beginning to end
I'll follow you.
(Ryan, aged 10)

I would like to thank the following: Hinchley Wood School, Esher, Surrey; Pearse House's "Lending Our Minds Out" courses; Sophie Chipperfield and Heybridge Junior School, Essex.

2. Excellence in the Teaching of Poetry

Fred Sedgwick

I have already made a statement about excellence in my chapter on the teaching of Shakespeare. Given that much of it holds equally true for this chapter, I will not repeat it here but readers are encouraged to refer back to it as they read what I have to say on the teaching of poetry. Some readers may feel that the previous chapter has too much theory but it is theory that I think is important: excellence is not a simple matter. It is both complex and problematic. This chapter is different. It is meant to be as practical as a cookbook. It sets out certain standing orders for excellence in teaching poetry and creative writing generally. These orders comprise the equivalent of the cookbook's section on what equipment the good kitchen needs: they are the kitchen's pots and pans, its utensils. This chapter also suggests practical ways in which good writing can be achieved: recipes, more or less.

I first heard the phrase 'standing order' twenty-five years ago, during my attendance at conferences of the National Union of Teachers. Standing orders were the rules governing procedure in debate. They could only be suspended under exceptional circumstances. By standing orders, I mean the principles that obtain in all lessons when we want children to write freshly, honestly and vigorously. I think that these standing orders are worth using until they are part of the working tradition of a classroom, or a school. Once these standing orders are part of the atmosphere which children breathe, use of them will enrich their writing enormously. One by-product of that enrichment, following after a lapse of time as surely as pudding follows the main course, will be a rise in what the government calls 'standards', those statistics of varying reliability. The first 'standing order' comes from the modernist poet, Pound (1954).

- Make it new

The quotation is worth seeing in its context:

Tching prayed on the mountain and
wrote MAKE IT NEW
on his bathtub ...

Sergei Diaghilev once told the writer and director Jean Cocteau *'etonne-moi'*: 'astonish me' (Fowlie, 1956). This is the same modernist thought. The writers and artists who were at the forward edge of the modernist movement – Diaghilev, the ballet designer; Cocteau, the writer; Picasso, the painter; Eliot and Pound, the poets; Joyce, the novelist; to take just six examples – all saw the need to say things in a way that surprised, astonished, even shocked.

In the classroom, this rule is useful. Children need to understand that their writing has to be theirs. They need to understand that it is better that writing should be strange than that it should be true. Writing is no use at all if it has been said before. I used to say to children: 'Alan will think of things that Mark won't think of, and Mark will think of things that Samantha won't think of ...' and so on. I introduce the notion of plagiarism. I ask a child: 'Can I steal your watch?', and when she replies with an indignant 'No!', I tell the class that they may not steal each other lines, either. When a child contributes something fresh to the preparatory discussion that precedes all writing lessons, I always praise it highly. 'That's yours, Samantha – make a note of that, on paper or in your head ... no one else can have that idea, it is Samantha's only ...' I suppose I could simply say to children, 'astonish me'. Often, we can help children to 'make it new' by emphasising metaphors, which are evidence of writers seeing similarities between otherwise disparate objects. I have written before about this (2001) that:

poetry, in its metaphorical behaviour, is always a link between two apparently disparate things: between, as I have said, the known and the unknown; also between two known things that, before, have never been seen to be connected. It is probably something of a cliché to say that, therefore, poetry is like an electrical spark, jumping creatively; with effects beyond the writer's immediate expectations and intentions.

Here are some children playing with simile, and thereby making something new:

My hamster
climbs
on the top of the cage
like a fireman
rescuing a child
from a building
on fire.
(Demi-Rae, aged 8)

I have a fish
that floats around
in the tank
like a bit of rubbish
on the top of the river.
(Georgina, aged 8)

My guinea pig
goes around
her spinning wheel
like washing
in a washing machine
(Louis, aged 8)

My dog tries to get out of the bath
like a wrestler in a fight.
(Kane, aged 8)

Those words conjure up a delightful picture of domestic mayhem.

A hedgehog
makes a spiky ball
like
Roman shield
protecting himself.
(Grant, aged 8)

My snake wiggles
like a shoelace
and stretches

when it stops
like a shoelace
all straight.
(Cheri, aged 8)

My snake
hisses
like
running water.
(Jed, aged 8)

I heard a lion
roaring
like a woman shouting
on a rock.
(David, aged 8; see Figure 2.1)

Figure 2.1:   'I heard a lion ...'

The recipe for this lesson is as follows:

- Ask the children to visualise an animal they know well. Get them to close their *physical* eyes, and make the animal do certain typical things in their minds, while looking at it with what Hamlet calls their '*minds*' eyes, what we might call their imaginations.
- Ask the children: What does the animal look like/resemble/remind you of as it does these things: moving, eating, drinking, sleeping, biting, licking, purring, barking?
- Do not let the children put their hands up. While they keep their eyes closed, ask them to think of other things the animal does, and what it looks like then. Go on like this for as long as possible. The objective is to get the children to pack their heads with words that are appropriate to your demands. Keep emphasising the words: 'like' 'remind' and 'resemble' in their simile-inducing mode. Keep emphasising that they should 'make it new'.
- When it feels right, ask the children for their contributions, and praise them all, unless, of course, they are clichés or plagiarisms. Be as hard as you dare on those. Get them to write their fresh phrases down in little poems like the examples quoted above.

I like linking drawing to writing, because, other things being equal, children who can draw with fluency are likely to be able to write fluently too. The drawings (see Figure 2.2) by Thomas, aged 8, are Thurberesque to my eyes and have a clear relationship with his writing.

Another way to help children to make things new is by combining two ways of writing. This next poem is both a *kenning* and a pair of *haiku*:

Natural fountain,
valley of flotsam – jetsam,
a storm of its own,

dark, full of mystery,
a motorway for seal life,
a slab of turquoise.
(Filip, aged 11)

A *kenning* is a poem that is a list of things you might call something: a list of epithets. Once again, the recipe simply involves the children closing their

My rabbit Jumps
up like a Jack
in a box.

my brid Flys
like a colful
brid feathr

my Cat stands
up like furry
monster.

by Thomas mustafe

Figure 2.2:   Drawing to writing

eyes, and thinking of names that they might give to anything you suggest: a globe, the sea, the moon, a pair of scissors, a human head, an ear. Or, they could keep their eyes open, and stare at examples of these objects, if, like the globe, the head and the scissors, they are present in the classroom. Ask them to think of two or three epithets before they put their hands up. Have a few of your own on hand in case they are slow at first. A pair of scissors, for example, might be coined as 'a sharp dancer capable of the splits'. The moon, famously, was, for Alfred Noyes, 'a ghostly galleon' (*The Highwayman*). Michael Laskey (1999) has a *kenning* poem about the human head, *Heads: Studies for a Self-Portrait* in which he describes it as, amongst many other things, 'A purse with small change and a bobble of fluff /A planet I'm planning one day to land on …' Then collect the children's suggestions, and get them to write them down.

A *haiku* is a poem that has 17 syllables, usually (but not always) arranged like this: 5 in the first line, 7 in the second and 5 in the third (Sedgwick, 2000b). Filip wrote his poem when I asked him and his classmates to find a list of epithets for water, and then, after some drafting, to arrange them in *haiku* form. The children were involved in a topic on water at the time, and were therefore surrounded by watery pictures, including *Seaport with the*

Embarkation of the Queen of Sheba by Claude Lorrain, Suerat's *Bathers at Asniers*, *A Lady in a Garden taking Coffee with some Children* by Nicolas Lancret and *The Thames Below Westminster* by Claude-Oscar Monet. All these powerful images contributed to this poem, and to other poems in this chapter. The second 'standing order' is

- Writing takes more than one draft

Look at this page of notes by Jenny (aged, 11; see Figure 2.3):

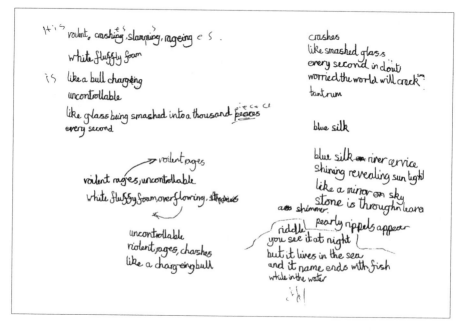

Figure 2.3:   Draft notes

What has been learned between the two sheets? It is worth examining this work to see what phrases have been added and discarded from the first draft, and to see how Jenny's feelings of confidence about initial jottings have helped her make her neat little verses (Figure 2.4). Writing on plain paper helps. It can be limiting for children to think of what they see as good ideas, and then to have to write them down on rules narrow feint paper, thus moving a measly inch down the page after half an hour's serious thought. Being taught not to worry about spelling mistakes in the initial stages helps, too.

uncontrollable
voilent, rages, charges
like a chargeing bull

by
  Jenny Wilson

        Aged 11   East Berghott

  crashes
  like smashed glass
  every second in dout
  worried the world will crack
   tantrum.

---

blue silk river surface
shineing revealing sun light
like a mirror sky
stone is throughn leaves a shimmer.   thrown
pearly ripples appear.

    by Jenny Wilson
        age 11
            East Berghott primary school

    Riddle
  you see it at night
  but it lives in the sea
  and its name ends with fish
  while in the water.

Figure 2.4:   Neat little verses

Children in this school had been taught not to use erasers in their writing, because rubbing words out wastes time, and encourages a view of writing that suggests it must be perfect at the first attempt. Any writer will know that this is an impossibility. Erasers in drawing, similarly, encourage children to aim at a photographic view in their presentation of reality: a view, of course, less than two hundred years old, and therefore not blessed by, for example, the great artists of the Renaissance, and therefore not worth blessing by us. The third 'standing order' is

- There are two aspects to all writing, secretarial and compositional

Wealthy writers do not have to consider the secretarial aspects of their job. The ease with which Noel Coward, for example, divided the compositional aspects of his work (which he did by himself) and the secretarial aspects (which someone else usually did for him), should alert us to an important question: are we, in any given lesson, teaching composition or secretarial skills? I am concerned here with the *former*. This is not to say that spelling, conventional grammar and legible handwriting are not important. But if a child writes something from her heart about a moment at home that moved her to tears of joy or sadness, it is callous to point out her secretarial errors. I should like to make this point with a poem of my own, based on a child's experience:

Kelly Jane's news January 8th

Our babby bruther jams michel
was born on chrismas day
and I rote about it in my news

but all my teecher did
was put in capitals and full stops
and corect my spelling

The fourth 'standing order' is

- There is more than one way to compose

Children use their own handwriting. This is overwhelmingly the most common way children write in schools. But there are other ways, rarely used.

They can, for example, use dictation to classroom helpers. This is valuable for those children whose heads are full of ideas, but who do not possess the wherewithal of getting them on to paper. Children can also use the computer as a compositional tool. This is almost never used in schools, as far as I can see, for composition, for the making of poems and stories. It is more often used as an aid to display, which is a different matter altogether. They can also dictate to the tape recorder: a method I have seldom seen used. The fifth 'standing order' is

- Make sure that the five senses are fully employed

The best way to do this is to ensure that children regularly write in the grip of firsthand experience (that is almost worthy of the status of a standing order on its own, but here it is to be part of another one). What follows are notes of mine following a session teaching children at Castle Acre Priory in Norfolk. I think that my recipes are implicit in the writing, so I am not going to spell them out.

> The children look poorly; one clutches her jaw, as if with toothache; another seems to be about to vomit at the feet of the holder of the camera; another has tightened her hood round her head to reveal only the centre of her face: narrowed eyes, wrinkled nose, queasy mouth (she needs to protect herself, it seems, from the elements: a cold drizzly day in March, 2000).
>
> We crowd them into the old Norman infirmary (hence the acting ill), line them up against the ruined wall, and take a photograph. Minutes later, dramatically recovered, the girls walk round the cloisters, pretending to be monks from nine centuries ago (see Plate 2.1). The silence is palpable at this point: the chatter is stilled, and the only sound is the birds singing over eastern England, as they have for centuries before these children were born.
>
> The children had spent half a day at Castle Acre Priory in Norfolk. This is a religious building that dates from the years just after the Norman invasion in 1066. It fell into ruin after it was closed in 1537 and later parts of it were used as barns and other farm buildings by the Victorians. The priory's substantial remains include the elaborately decorated west front of the church and the prior's lodging and chapel. Both of these largely survived the various crises the building went through. Aspects of the monks' lives are reflected in a cupboard to be

Plate 2.1:   The old Norman infirmary

found in one of the church walls and in the stone benches of the chapter house where they sat daily for meetings. Looking through archways, doorways and windows, we have little difficulty in imagining the life of the monks who lived here. We were pleased, but not surprised, to find that the children did not have many problems imagining either.

Looking through archways, doorways and windows was one of the things that we asked the children to do as they walked around. The effect of this exercise was to frame objects – clouds, ruins, trees, the village church half a mile away, and make the children look harder. Sometimes, an archway framed another archway, which in turn framed wintry trees and the surrounding countryside. We were trying to make the children look (as Blake said we all should) 'until it hurts'. 'The world is', as a modern poet, George Tardios, wrote 'troubled with a lack of looking' (Pirrie, 1987):

Through the arches I can see
acres and acres of fields.
Through the arches I could see
monks killing animals.

Plate 2.2:   Through the arches

Through the arches I can see
the Priory staring at me.
Through the arches I could see
monks going to the brewery.
Through the arches I can see
big tall pillars.
Through the arches I could see
monks baking bread.
Through the arches I can see
a stream flowing to the sea.
Through the arches I could see
monks working in the fields.
(Matthew, aged 10)

I looked through the bottom archway
and saw stones, pointy flint stones,
piled up on each other.

I looked through the top archway
and saw clouds moving in a blue sky.

I looked through the archway long ago
and saw monks praying on their knees
singing hymns in Latin
walking slowly and silently in a single file
taking wine up to the first east end.
(A joint composition by Adam, Charlotte, Jordan, aged 7, 8 and 7)

In both of these examples, the repeated phrase – 'Through the arches I can see' and 'I looked through the archway' has acted like a writing frame (as the National Literacy Strategy Framework for Teaching puts it) and has set the writers at ease to make their observations real on paper.

'Look at these walls. What do they look like? What do they remind you of? What do they resemble?' It was important to spend fifteen minutes doing two teaching tasks before we did the exercises described above: first, getting the children into the mood of the place, and second, getting them into the way of thinking about similes. Later this work paid off as the children wrote about the first part of the priory that they had encountered:

The wall felt knobbly and crumbly like dog biscuits (Jade, aged 8) … They looked like snakes' scales (Roza, aged 10) … like ripped paper (Poppy, aged 9) … like flint arrow heads, spear blades and axe ends too … like a jumbled-up puzzle, broken pictures, ripped-up mosaics (Thomas, aged 8) … like muesli, a clay separated pot, horses' hooves

The walls of the barn remind me of
    vegetable curry
    crumbly potatoes
    crisps falling out of a packet
    crumbly crumbs falling from biscuit
    lumps of chocolate with icing cake chopped up
(Daniel, aged 8)

The windows looked like an ace of diamonds but black instead of red (Roza, aged 8)

The wonderful west door confronted us, interlocking arches 'carved like barley sugar twists' (as one of the teachers wrote later). This is an awesome sight. Unlike most of the original building, much of it has survived. Only the roof is completely gone, and we asked the children to imagine this structure as it was, protected from the rain that was, that day, so unfriendly. Some of the lower arches are pure, early Norman – round and decorated in a basic way. As you look higher and higher, you see more and more decoration: intricate little triangles around the half-circles. Higher up still, there are the pointed arches of the Early Gothic.

We walk around the rest of the priory. Has the idea of similes taken hold?

> The ruins looked like Medusa's hair on a bad day and the roof of the
> porch looked like tangled vines
> (Roza, aged 8)

> The trees look like weeping sticks and the clouds look like whipped
> cream
> The pouring rain
> and the growling wind
> are the cause of the crumbling structure …
> Decaying teeth and jagged rocks
> All remind me of this broken paradise.
> (Sam, aged 10)

> The arches reminded me of cats' arched backs and the patterns on the
> walls looked like old coat racks … The steep spiral staircase made me
> think of an ever-growing flower, and the ceiling of the porch looked
> like bending train tracks.
> (Lauren, aged 11)

It had worked. Even the youngest children wrote vividly:

> I can see my face in the glittering well.
> I can see a plant in the glittering well.
> I can see a bird flying over the glittering well.
> I can see some ruins around the glittering well.
> (Charlie, aged 7)

Here the repetition, so natural to young writers, made a satisfying poem. In all this work, two connected elements contributed towards its success. One was a reminder to use the five senses, and the other was the first hand nature of the experience.

Sometimes, of course, children have to write under the influence of a second hand experience. This boy was studying ancient Egypt, and had looked at photographs of the Nile. His poem is, of course, a *tanka* (a poem with 31 syllables in the following pattern: 5, 7, 5, 7, 7).

Lonely feluccas
Ride the serene River Nile
Pushing through the weeds
Viewing the scenic backdrop
Watching glistening ripples.
(Peter, aged 11)

Jessica's *cinquain* (a poem with 22 syllables in the following pattern: 2, 4, 6, 8, 2) was written while looking at a reproduction of Suerat's *Bridge at Ansieres*. This is partly a second hand experience – she was not looking at the river – but partly a first hand one insofar as she was looking at the painting of the river:

Water
gushing shimmer
vibrant rays of rainbow
sparkling still liquid calmly drops
water
(Jessica, aged 10)

This poem was written whilst examining David Hockney's *Portrait of Nick Wilder*:

This water
feels
like smooth
blue icing.
It sounds
like water
lapping

the slate tiles.
It tastes
like smooth
clothes
that have
just
been ironed.
This water
looks like
sapphires tumbling
down
foaming
cliffs
round and round
in the sunlight.
(Geoffrey, aged 10)

This poem could have fitted within other standing orders. It is evidence of using the senses as a stimulus, and it was composed, not with handwriting, but on a computer.

Art often helps children to write. David was 11 years old when he studied a blue period Picasso painting in reproduction of a sad young woman. He wrote the poem below. (The recipe had included the idea of pattern: make sure that there is a repeated phrase in your poem.)

I saw her standing
all alone
nothing there
but her long cloak

I saw her standing
all alone
nothing there
but the red rose

I saw her standing
all alone
nothing there
but the shadow of the boat

I saw her standing
all alone
nothing there
but the dark blue sea

I saw her standing
all alone
nothing there
but the sleeping baby.

The sixth 'standing order' is

- Verbs come first, nouns second, and adjectives and adverbs nowhere

Children need to learn that verbs are the most vital (that is, living) elements in their language. This is because they actually move things, like 'dash', and 'hobble' and 'run' and 'walk' and 'creep' and 'slither'. Or they stop things: like 'stop' itself, or 'halt'. Or they change things: 'alter', 'transmogrify', 'change' itself. Playing thesaurus games with verbs is useful and enjoyable.

Nouns come next in importance, because, representing things and people, they have a necessary presence. Adjectives and adverbs are less important than teachers often think. Children asked to think of some 'nice, exciting adjectives to make their stories more interesting' are being given advice that will, if taken, kill their writing. Take two passages:

He felt very depressed, walking sadly along the dark, rainy street that gloomy winter, with the ugly, polluted river surging dramatically against its banks ...

He walked once through a rainy night ...

The first tells us everything the writer wants us to know about the man, leaving us no room for our own contribution. The paradox is, the writing is meant to convey emotion – but it has less emotional impact on us as readers in the long run. The second passage, stripped of all adjectives and adverbs, allows us as readers to bring our own experiences to bear on the story.

What about the poetry that we should be reading or reciting to children? Reading poetry to children on a regular basis is often squeezed out. How can children write poems when they have no idea what a poem is? We might as well ask them to make something that moves across the table with the help of elastic bands and cotton reels, without them ever having seen a car or a bus or a train or a bike. If we want children to write well, we should expose them daily to poetry. I could easily list here the poets that I think children should not miss. But I would rather list some criteria for choosing poetry:

- Does the poem look as if it was written only for children? You know what I mean. It is all about bums and pimples, or uses contemporary slang that will be out of date inside a decade. This sort of poetry is deeply conservative and patronising. If children want poetry about bums and pimples (and they do) they will make it up themselves on the playground. Leave them to it.
- If the poem is a good poem for adults as well as children you are on surer ground. The great writer Charles Causley has written some-where that he is never sure when he begins a poem whether it is for adults or for children.
- If a given poem seems to give up its meaning at one reading, it is probably not good enough, for children or for adults. Truth is always more complex than an advertising slogan might suggest.

Here are some traditional poems worth trying with children, all of which can be found in Sedgwick (2000a):

Meet me in the green glen by John Clare
If ever I should by chance grow rich by Edward Thomas
My cat Jeoffry by Christopher Smart
Pied Beauty by Gerard Manley Hopkins
My baby has a mottled fist by Christina Rossetti

I wish to thank East Bergholt Primary School and Greensted Junior School for their help.

3. Approaching Text Through Drama

Judith Ackroyd and Jo Boulton

'There's something empowering for young children about drama. It's about learning and problem-solving in their world.'

'We regularly plan drama as part of our literacy learning and have used drama particularly successfully to promote writing in Reception.'

These words were spoken by Angie Matthews, an English co-ordinator in a lower school, during an interview with her. She had found that drama activities not only help to fulfil the National Curriculum and National Literacy Strategy criteria for teaching English but also excite children about their learning and encourage them to look more closely at written and oral texts.

This chapter sets out to give guidance on the kinds of drama techniques and strategies which will help teachers to achieve the excellent results and enthusiasm for teaching which Angie clearly enjoys. It will also discuss the point that despite the higher priority now given to drama in the programmes of study for English in the National Curriculum 2000, there is a continuing criticism in OFSTED inspections (DfEE/QCA, 1999: 181) that not enough drama is being taught in primary schools.

An important part of the chapter is a lesson plan using Tennyson's classic narrative poem, *The Lady of Shalott.* It is made up of a series of dramatic activities which are easy for the teacher to follow. After a description of each activity, there is an analysis explaining why each technique is used, and how it relates to the National Curriculum for English. The lesson plan demonstrates how a drama-based approach to the poem can offer a range of opportunities for children to achieve excellence in oral work, reading and writing.

Teachers may use the lesson plan in its entirety, or may choose to select specific drama techniques to apply to different teaching contexts.

The implications of drama in the statutory curriculum

The consequences of drama now being a compulsory element of the English National Curriculum are significant and will inevitably necessitate changes in the practices of many primary classroom teachers. Let us look at the implications in turn and then suggest ways forward to address the new teaching requirements.

Drama can no longer be avoided

Since 1989 teachers have had to respond to various government demands, initiatives, and new teaching guidelines, the most recent being the National Curriculum Orders in England and Wales (2000). These require teachers to include drama in their teaching of English. Drama is also referred to in the objectives of the framework for teaching in the National Literacy Strategy (DfEE, 1998). Therefore, no longer can the decision to use drama be merely at the whim of the individual teacher. Since September 2000 the place of drama in the National Curriculum for English has been cemented and extended. Drama now has its statutory position. Within the speaking and listening (En1) programmes of study at Key Stage 1 and 2, drama activities are included in 'knowledge, skills and understanding' and are also exemplified in the 'range of activities, contexts and purposes'. Children are required to develop an understanding of the written forms of drama as writers, readers and performers. At Key Stage 1 (DfEE/QCA, 2000: 44), pupils have to learn to:

a use language and actions to explore and convey situations, characters and emotions;

b create and sustain roles individually and when working with others;

c comment constructively on drama they have watched or in which they have taken part.

These objectives will be achieved through working in role, presenting drama and stories to others and responding to performances. At Key Stage 2 pupils will 'participate in a wide range of drama activities and evaluate their own and others' contributions' (51-2) through:

a   improvisation and working in role;
b   scripting and performing in plays;
c   responding to performances.

These specific requirements ensure a drama entitlement for all children, constituting evidence that drama is officially acknowledged as an essential strategy to achieve excellence in English teaching.

Drama terminology must be learned and understood

It is worth noting that the terminology used to describe drama activities is more specific than in previous National Curriculum documentation and that the examples given correspond to the metalanguage of drama education, for instance, 'hot-seating', 'tableaux' and 'flashbacks'. It is assumed that all teachers will know this terminology and understand how to use the techniques in the classroom, just as they would be expected to know how to help children improve their writing through knowing and using the metalanguage of grammar. It is now an expectation that such knowledge is or should be part of every teacher's vocabulary, understanding and teaching repertoire. An understanding of nouns, verbs and complex sentences gives teachers the knowledge base that enables them to teach about language effectively and to help children achieve excellence in using language in a variety of contexts. Similarly, a teacher who is confident with the terminology and techniques of drama will be able to use it to maximise children's learning opportunities in English.

Drama is recommended in the National Literacy Strategy

In addition to the statutory requirements of the National Curriculum, there are explicit references to drama in the National Literacy Strategy Framework for Teaching. In Year 1, term 1, for example, children will 're-enact stories in a variety of ways, e.g. through role play, using dolls or puppets' (DfEE, 1998: 20). In Year 5, term 1, text level work objective 5, 'pupils should be taught to understand dramatic conventions including: the conventions of scripting, how character can be communicated in words and gesture, how tension can be built up through pace, silences and delivery' (44). In module

5 of the "Lunchbox" (DES, 1998: 7) training materials, drama is highlighted as a teaching strategy and not just an end in itself: 'Drama techniques play an important role within and beyond the literacy hour as a means of responding to a text.' Therefore, the National Literacy Strategy promotes the use of drama to achieve its aims of raising standards in English.

Curriculum planning must include drama

Given its firm place in the National Curriculum Orders for English and in the National Literacy Strategy, why is it that drama is not already a regular experience for children in the primary classroom? It was noted by Robinson, (1999: 181) that:

> OFSTED inspections suggest that too few schools teach drama. Drama receives little attention in primary school inspection reports, but such references as there are, confirm its importance. In Key Stages 1-3 provision for drama is poor because of its low status and low levels of funding. Objectives are unclear, teachers lack confidence in teaching it, and practice varies between classes in the same school.

There are many reasons for this. Teaching has undergone such relentless change over the last decade and a half that teachers have been overwhelmed with new initiatives, paperwork and regulations with the consequence that many have simply not been able to keep pace with the range of new techniques and knowledge across so many different subject areas. Set against a continual treadmill of competing curricula and pressures of accountability, teaching drama may understandably have been perceived as a low priority.

The time and organisational constraints of the National Literacy Strategy and the imposed structure of the literacy hour, followed in most schools, may have sometimes led to less varied and creative teaching methods in literacy teaching. However, these should not be seen as excuses for avoiding using drama. Indeed, the National Literacy Strategy training materials specify that teachers should use a wide range of teaching strategies, and as previously noted, drama must be one of those strategies. It is an excellent teaching strategy for promoting and demonstrating the inter-relatedness of the three language modes: speaking and listening, reading, and writing.

In order to cope with the planning of new schemes of work necessary to meet the national literacy objectives, some schools have purchased published schemes, which contain few or sometimes no drama suggestions. Until very recently there was a serious shortage of suitable material offering suggestions of how drama can be used in the strategy. In a climate of 'big books' domination, text has usually been interpreted as written text, obscuring the possibility of text as an oral text. A written text often appears to be the safe option with its carefully constructed form, along with easily identifiable objectives and suggestions in the support materials for follow-up work.

Unlike the written text, an oral text created within a dramatic improvisation is ephemeral. The words are not pre-determined; indeed the drama text is unpredictable since the children are the authors of the text. They construct the text at the same time as they read whilst de-constructing and interpreting the text. Individuals create the oral drama text together as a group. The text created will not be predictable since the children generate it themselves and indeed there are possibilities for some exciting and refreshing outcomes. It is in these spontaneous and unexpected moments that excellence can emerge. Therefore, drama experiences need to be included in regular planning.

There is a need to overcome fears and be flexible

A further implication is the need for flexibility in teaching style, especially given the widely held fear of drama within the teaching profession. We have been asked questions such as: 'Will it lead to chaos in my classroom?' 'How can I keep control when the children are all over the place?' 'How can I remain in charge when I am pretending to be someone else?' 'How can I do drama when I'm too embarrassed?' It is not uncommon for teachers to feel that drama might not be much more than recreation for the children, or worse, simply messing about. There may also be teachers who adopt a view that children may not be able to cope with the sort of freedom involved in drama activities, and they fear it carries with it a potential for chaos and consequent loss of control. Many teachers base their understandings of what drama is on their own experiences at primary school. Christmas nativity plays, BBC radio broadcasts, 'being' a snowflake or a tree! (Kitson and Spiby, 1995: 1-2). It is perhaps the unfamiliarity of drama classroom practice that leads to fears. These fears can be overcome when the drama process is understood, which is why time is given to analysis in the lesson plan later in the chapter. Teachers need to try out drama activities for themselves in order to discover their intrinsic pedagogic value, and their powers to intrigue, entice and motivate children.

Drama training is needed

In the past and indeed even now, teacher training has not prepared teachers adequately for using drama as a teaching strategy nor as performance art. Both aspects of drama are important and the National Curriculum requires children to take part in and respond to performances as well as to participate in classroom drama. The two are not mutually exclusive and in fact develop different kinds of skill, knowledge and understanding. Indeed, the lesson plan provided includes both aspects of drama practice. It is interesting to note that OFSTED pointed to a positive relationship between a school's arts provision and its achievement in literacy (Robinson, 1999): 'Her Majesty's Inspectorate said that "there is a positive correlation between good provision/performance in the arts in schools and higher standards of performance in literacy and numeracy according to OFSTED inspection statistics".'

We should look to drama practitioners and researchers

To reassure the reader who may be anxious about using drama, it is important to be aware of the historical perspective and the dramatic growth in the field. The Drama-in-Education movement emerged in the United Kingdom in the 1950s through the energy and commitment of Slade (1954) and Way (1967). During the 1960s and 1970s Heathcote (1979) and Bolton (1979) developed new possibilities through the use of the teacher-in-role approach to drama teaching. This approach engaged the teacher in fictional roles with the children. Drama has continued to develop both as a learning strategy in the primary school and a discrete subject at the secondary phase. The growth of drama education has been strongly influenced by the inspirational practice and writing of practitioners such as Neelands (1984), Neelands and Goode (2000), O'Neill and Lambert (1982), and O'Neill (1995) whose work has continually made theory relevant to the classroom. Two significant United Kingdom drama associations for teachers are National Drama (ND); the National Association for Teachers of Drama (NATD), and the National Association for Teachers of English (NATE) which has a significant focus on drama in its constitution and within its range of publications. However, the United Kingdom is no longer the sole focus of development in drama. Drama education now boasts international status. At regular international conferences drama teachers share their practice. The International Drama in Education Institute (IDIERI) began in Brisbane,

Australia in 1995 with twenty delegates. The third gathering in Ohio, United States of America, in 2000 drew one hundred and forty people. Delegates to the International Drama Education Association (IDEA) conferences number into the thousands.

Drama teachers' magazines and research journals are now published all over the world. In the early 1980s it was possible to know every book published in the field of drama education. By 2000 it was a struggle to keep up with those published in the United Kingdom alone. The rapid growth of drama education gave rise to some interesting research on drama practice for learning in English. For example, Booth and Neelands (1998) provided, in classroom projects connecting writing and drama, twelve examples of dramas, drawn from practitioners across the globe, that have been used to stimulate writing activities, many of them in fictional contexts. Ackroyd's (2000) work contains dramas specifically designed to explore the learning objectives in the National Literacy Strategy Framework for Teaching. Drama education is developing, practice is theorised, researched and expressed through publications, conferences and in professional associations worldwide. Clearly, drama in education is not a mere 'flash in the pan'. It has its own theoretical base underpinning its practice. Further publications about teaching drama can be found in the References at the end of the book.

Opportunities for excellence in the classroom

We have looked at the implications of the inclusion of drama in the statutory requirements for English and have acknowledged some of the reservations teachers have about drama. We will now consider the benefits of using drama to achieve excellence in the English classroom. The drama plan based on Tennyson's poem, *The Lady of Shalott*, is for Key Stage 2 pupils. It has been chosen to demonstrate how a classic poem can be explored using a range of drama techniques. The poem is intriguing for its mysterious setting, fascinating for its lack of resolve and orally exciting for its vocabulary and rhythm. ('The range [of literature] should include classic poetry' DfEE, 2000: 54). During the course of the lesson children are given various tasks the purpose of which is to provide rich, varied and active ways of studying the poem. For example, they create images to accompany lines of the poem, give formal readings of sections, consider genre and its impact for different presentations of the story line, as well as engage in improvised discussion about the Lady of Shalott's death.

This lesson plan provides opportunities for children actively to:

- investigate a classic text;
- explore and interpret the meaning of the poem;
- consider the mood generated by the text;
- listen to the teacher reading sections of the poem;
- prepare readings of selected lines;
- perform text;
- interrogate implications of genre;
- appreciate the rhythm, pace and sounds of the poem;
- reflect on the impact of aspects of the poem's structure;
- use the language of feelings and emotion;
- contextualise and activate language;
- explore and understand characters and situations;
- use language for different purposes;
- sequence and predict.

This list demonstrates how one lesson plan can cover a huge range of learning opportunities, which are, moreover, demanding and challenging. In these activities children will develop speaking and listening, reading and writing skills within a literary and interactive context. Teachers will want to make their own decisions on whether children need particular teaching points clarified but it should be possible to teach this lesson just as it is set out below. After each activity is described in the lesson plan, an analysis of the rationale and process will follow to indicate how children can be encouraged and enabled to find their own level of excellence in English. Although this lesson plan has an English focus as indicated above, it also offers a range of other learning possibilities, such as working as part of a group and respecting and valuing the ideas of others. This dramatic approach to exploring the poem has been carefully constructed with non-drama specialists in mind. The activities are highly structured, tightly organised and unthreatening for both teacher and children. What they offer is an engaging, active and varied approach to making a poetic text accessible.

The lesson plan: *The Lady of Shalott*

Age group   9-11 years
Resources   Tennyson's *The Lady of Shalott*

Activities

Activities are mostly carried out in small groups. The children can change or remain in the same groups throughout. The activities need to be run through in order. The order is a recommended one especially for those teachers who do not feel confident using drama. We do not tell the children that the poem is *The Lady of Shalott* by Lord Alfred Tennyson until the end of activity (4). Teachers may then choose to give a little information about the poet, but it is not necessary for the lesson plan. There is no reason why the children should not know the poem from the outset, but it adds to the mysterious atmosphere of the plan, and furthermore they are not put off by the idea of a classic poem.

Activity (1)   What is a romantic heroine? *(Class discussion)*

Invite discussion about what a romantic heroine would be like. It may be helpful to take the two words separately first. Some suggestions of women thought to be romantic heroines could be discussed, for example, Sleeping Beauty, Beauty in *Beauty and the Beast*, Shakespeare's Juliet.

- Activate prior learning, and individual cultural experiences and understandings

Through an informal mode of talk, children are given the opportunity to draw upon their own personal understandings which might be taken from books that they have read, the media, people they have met and/or stories they have heard. Inevitably, one child's romantic heroine will differ from another's. Herein lies the potential for discussion. The role of the teacher is to value all the contributions and to frame questions in such a way that will allow an open debate. Ideas are gathered, collected, and shared. The concept of the romantic heroine is broadened and made accessible to children with a range of different background experiences.

- Preparing to meet the Lady of Shalott

This discussion builds bridges into the text. It makes the children aware of one of the central themes of the poem before they even meet it.

Activity (2)   Physical image of a romantic heroine *(Small group sculpting)*

Sculpting is a very useful way 'of crystallising meaning into concrete images, a very economical and controlled form of expression as well as a sign to be interpreted or read by others' (Neelands and Goode, 2000).

It involves a child being 'moulded' by the other group members to depict their view of a romantic heroine. Sculptures can include more than one person and even objects. It does not matter of course, how funny or exaggerated they are at this stage. They can experiment with where the eyes should be looking, the tilt of the head, position of feet and hands etc.

- 'Physicalising' a concept to clarify meaning

Through negotiation, speculation and experimentation, the groups of children explore the ways in which the body can communicate ideas, feelings, and concepts. They have the opportunity to manipulate the physical image in order to express the vision of the romantic heroine upon which they have agreed.

To talk effectively as members of a group, pupils should be taught to:

a   make contributions relevant to the topic and take turns in discussion;
b   vary contributions to suit the activity and purpose, including exploratory and tentative comments where ideas are being collected together, and reasoned, evaluative comments as discussion moves to conclusions or actions.

The range of purposes should include planning, predicting, exploring. (DfEE/QCA, 2000: 50)

- Introduction to sculpting

This prepares children for the next activities in which children sculpt images to explore the text. It gives them the chance to understand how sculpting works, its possibilities and limitations.

Activity (3)   Re-organising the sculptures and poem extracts *(Small group discussion and reforming of sculptured image)*

Explain to the children that in the next activity they will be asked to re-form their sculptures and listen to some extracts of a poem. After each extract the groups discuss how they will amend their image to take into account the new information. Each extract could be displayed in written form after it has been read to enable the children to re-read to check the details.

Extract 1

> Four grey walls and four grey towers,
> Overlook a space of flowers

Here for example, groups may wish to represent the wall around the woman, the towers and/or the flowers. They use themselves as well as chairs if convenient.

Extract 2

> There she weaves by night and day
> A magic web with colours gay

Groups now consider how this will change their sculpture, and re-form it.

Extract 3

> And moving thro' a mirror clear
> That hangs before her all the year,
> Shadows of the world appear.

Again, each group considers how this may affect their sculpture and make any changes they choose. Some children may need help with these lines so that they understand the reference to the reflections in the mirror.

Extract 4

> Out flew the web and floated wide;
> The mirror cracked from side to side;
> 'The curse has come upon me,' cried
> The Lady of Shalott.

A final re-adjustment of the image is made in each group.

- 'Physicalising' meaning

Through negotiation, the children agree on how to present their sculptures.

- Listening to poetry read aloud by teacher

This gives the opportunity for the children to listen to lines of poetry read fluently and expressively. They are listening with a particular purpose since they know they have a task to complete.

- Introducing the text in manageable chunks

This is an easy and accessible way to introduce a long, fairly complex text. They are extracts from different parts of the poem selected to give an indication of the plot and atmosphere.

> Pupils should be taught to make connections between different parts of a text. (DfEE/QCA, 2000: 53)

- Close scrutiny of text

The task requires children to consider the meanings, atmosphere and implications created by the words. The need to understand the text, in turn, makes demands upon the children at each stage. Their understanding and shared interpretations of the lines they have heard are 're-presented' in a physical form. In the following activity their understandings are recalled and articulated through discussion, in verbal form:

> To listen, understand and respond appropriately to others, pupils should be taught to recall and re-present important features of … reading. (DfEE/QCA, 2000: 50)

Activity (4)   Making sense of the fragments *(Whole-class discussion)*

A shared reading of all the extracts with a discussion of interesting words and phrases that may need clarification, such as 'a magic web with colours gay'.
Ask the children what sense they have made of the lines, for example:

Who have we met in the poem?
What do you think is happening?
What do you think the setting might be of this poem?
What atmosphere was created?
Which words or phrases helped to create the atmosphere?
How did making the sculptures help you to understand the lines of the poem?

The children may wish to re-visit their sculptures and re-draft and edit them according to new understandings. The physical texts can be altered just as written texts.

- Clarifying collective understanding

The children's ideas and perceptions of the poem extracts are shared, considered, the text re-visited and conclusions made. It does not matter if the children's interpretations are not appropriate in the context of the whole poem. This is why their sculptures are not shared with the whole group:

> To listen, understand and respond appropriately to others, pupils should be taught to recall and re-present important features of ... reading. (DfEE/QCA, 2000: 50)

- Growing confidence in using the language of the poem

Through listening, reading, and the use of the lines in their group discussion children gain confidence and familiarity with Tennyson's work.

Activity (5)   Words in action *(Group presentation)*

Groups are given a copy of the extracts read above. Their task is to repeat the four sculptures they have created to depict the extracts, but this time they select a few words from each extract to accompany each of the sculptures. They need to rehearse how the words are said and should consider the following:

Volume
Speed
Pauses

They can decide whether they whisper, repeat, chant or even sing the words that are selected. They should then practise moving from one image to the next whilst saying the lines. Variations to this activity include:

using only one extract to work on with the one appropriate sculpture;
limiting some groups to particular words or phrases;
presentation of children's work.

After each performance discussion should focus on the effect of the chosen words and how they are spoken in relation to the sculpture. Some examples of the kinds of question the teacher could ask are listed below:

Which words do you remember the group using?
How were they spoken?
Which bits were louder than others?
What was the effect of the changing volume?
What mood did they create?
Are there any changes that could be made to emphasise the atmosphere?
How did the sound-scape relate to the sculpture?
What did the sculpture tell us?

• Selection of text

Through discussion and negotiation children choose words and phrases. These choices are based on their responses to the sound of the words, their texture and rhythm, as well as their meaning:

Pupils should be taught to use inference and deduction. (DfEE/QCA, 2000: 53)

• Experimenting with language

Children experiment with the way the words can be made to sound and how they might be uttered to correspond with the meaning of the words and to the particular sculpture. At the same time, they experiment with bringing words and phrases together which are not necessarily next to each other on the page. They match words and bring together oppositional phrases, making their own meaning through such juxta-positions as 'floated' and 'cracked' and the way they are pronounced. The effect of this is to make the children the poets. They use Tennyson's words, but they create the word order, significance and sounds to generate their own poetic moments:

> To develop understanding and appreciation of literary texts, pupils should be taught to recognise the choice, use and effect of figurative language, vocabulary and patterns of language. (DfEE/QCA, 2000: 53)

- Performing their own texts

Children enjoy performing their work and making it their own. An example is a group of children whispering 'floated' repeatedly. After a few whispers, one child shouts the word 'cracked' harshly breaking the atmosphere created by the soft repetition. Then the whispering children take on the word 'cracked', subverting it into a gentle sounding word.

The children can also layer the selected words or phrases by saying different words at the same time. The performance therefore communicates through the sculptured physical image, through the selected words themselves, and through the delivery of those words:

> To speak with confidence in a range of contexts, adapting their speech for a range of purposes and audiences, pupils should be taught to gain and maintain the interest and response of different audiences (for example, by exaggeration, humour, varying pace and using persuasive language to achieve particular effects). (DfEE/QCA, 2000: 50)

- Responding to performance

The choice of questions the teacher asks is vital to ensure that a mutually supportive and objective discourse ensues:

> To develop understanding and appreciation of literary texts, pupils should be taught to consider poetic forms and their effects. (DfEE/QCA, 2000: 53)

> To participate in a wide range of drama activities and to evaluate their own and others' contributions, pupils should be taught to evaluate how they and others have contributed to the overall effectiveness of performance in the NC ... (DfEE/QCA, 2000: 51)

To listen, understand and respond appropriately to others, pupils should be taught to identify features of language used for a specific purpose. (DfEE/QCA, 2000: 50)

Activity (6)   How will the story end? *(Small group predictions)*

Each group

discusses what has happened to the Lady of Shalott;
predicts how the narrative could end;
selects someone to report their prediction to the class.

The children base their prediction on the little snippets of text they have seen and heard as well as the atmosphere that has been created through their practical work:

Pupils should be taught to use inference and deduction ... look for meaning beyond the literal. (DfEE/QCA, 2000: 53)

Activity (7)   How the poem ends *(Small group mime and teacher reading)*

Teacher reads the final extract, and then gives the children a copy. In their groups, the children plan how they can provide actions to accompany the teacher's reading of the verse. A few of them can be the knights crossing themselves looking down at the boat as they read the lines, and they should discuss how Lancelot will look different and distinct from the others.

Who is this? And what is here?
And in the lighted palace near
Died the sound of royal cheer;
And they cross'd themselves for fear,
All the knights at Camelot:
But Lancelot mused a little space;
He said, 'She has a lovely face;
God in his mercy lend her grace,
The Lady of Shalott'.

Teacher then reads the verse aloud and each group performs at the same time. Some may choose to show the others their work.

- Listening

This is the first time the children listen to a whole verse read aloud. They are now familiar with the style, the language and the context of the poem. Now they are able to make some sense of hearing a whole verse. Again, the teacher will be modelling an expressive reading:

> The range should include opportunities for pupils to listen to live readings. (DfEE/QCA, 2000: 51)

- Close analysis of the text

In order to match the actions to the text, the children need to examine carefully the lines of the verse. The children, again, have a purpose for their reading:

> Pupils should be taught to obtain specific information through detailed reading. (DfEE/QCA, 2000: 53)

Activity (8)   The story is told (*Teacher in role*)

The purpose of this activity is to give the children the plot of the poem and access some of Tennyson's language. A narrative is provided which gives the gist of the story and includes various quotations. The children are asked to imagine that they live in or around Camelot. Teachers can, of course, choose their own way of approaching this part of the activity:

either:

The teacher takes on the role of an old woman from Camelot who reads to the class from her diary. She tells the class that she has been looking at the diary entry she wrote a year ago to the day. It makes her think about what a strange world it is. The diary entry recalls what took place in Camelot a year ago and tells of the rumours surrounding a very strange incident.

At times throughout the reading the teacher as the old lady asks whether the children have any questions. For example, do they believe her? Have they heard similar rumours about the story? These questions will have the effect of breaking up the narrative and ensure an understanding of what has been read. Some suggestions for other questions to ask the children are provided in the text of the narrative poem.

or:

In this approach the teacher needs to be familiar with the narrative before she begins so that she can tell it as a story rather than read it as an imaginary diary. She is an old lady who wants to share her memories of a strange incident with the children. She tells them what she remembers. It is important for the teacher to include some of the quotations taken from the poem. Questions can be asked in the same way to help sustain the interest and active involvement of the children.

> 'It was all so strange. No one even knew for sure that anyone lived in the four grey walls and four grey towers on the little island. My husband was a reaper then, and he said they used to hear someone singing when they were out reaping early among the bearded barley in the morning. They used to have a joke that some half believed and others wanted to believe that there was a "Fairy Lady of Shalott" up in the casement window, high up in one of the towers. It's strange to think that so many people passed that way down to tower'd Camelot, and yet nobody ever saw her.'

>> You must have passed by there sometimes. Did you ever look up at the casement window?
>> Were any of you reapers? Did you hear the singing from the tower?
>> Do you think people called her a fairy lady as a joke or did they really think there was something magical or mysterious about her?

> 'Some time after she was found dead in the boat, people from Camelot went up to her room and they couldn't believe what they found there. There was a loom, a magic web with colours gay, and many weaved pictures of scenes that she must have seen from the window. But remember that she was never, ever seen looking out of

the window. I have heard a whisper say, a curse is on her if she stay
to look down to Camelot. So until this day, she never did look out to
Camelot. They soon found out how she was able to see who passed
by. There was a huge mirror. But here is the oddest thing. The
mirror was cracked. Not just cracked, but crack'd from side to side.
Those who went to the room said there was a very mournful
atmosphere in the room. They felt a strange power in there. It was
almost as though there was some magic in the room.'

>   Did any of you go into the tower?
>   How would you describe the atmosphere?
>   Would it really have been possible for her to see what went on
>   outside through the mirror?
>   Could it have been a practical joke after all there are a lot of
>   youngsters around with a strange sense of humour these days!

'Now, you may have heard about this curse. Of course no one knows
why there should have been a curse on such a beautiful young lady,
nor what exactly the curse could have been. One thing is certain. The
curse came upon her the day that Lancelot passed by. You may have
heard about him. He was one of King Arthur's Knights of the Round
Table. Well, many folk say that she saw the reflection of him riding
past in the mirror. The bridle bells rang merrily as he rode down to
Camelot. The helmet and the helmet feather burn'd like one burning
flame together. She couldn't help herself. She turned to look directly
through the window. It was this that seems to have brought about her
fate. There are those who were on the river that day who swear they
heard the mirror crack and tear apart as it crashed and fell in splinters
to the ground.'

>   Did any of you see Sir Lancelot? Was he so good looking to turn
>   a poor girl's head?
>   Did any of you hear the crash of the mirror?

'They saw her leave the towers, looking so calm, as though she was
in a trance. She was dressed in a snowy white robe. Down she came
and found a boat beneath a willow left afloat. That was an odd
coincidence. It was as though the boat was meant to be there for her.
Round about the prow she wrote "The Lady of Shallot". In the boat

she floated down to Camelot. Can you imagine what a sight it was! You may wonder why nobody approached her. She had an air of mystery about her. Poor girl. They heard her singing her last song. Can you believe that she sang as she lay in that boat? Sang, that is until her blood was frozen slowly.

As people gathered around the boat they were afraid and crossed themselves to keep any bad spirits away. That's how mysterious the whole thing was. As for Sir Lancelot, well, all he had to say was, "She has a lovely face. God in his mercy, lend her grace, The Lady of Shalott". I don't know what to make of any of it.'

> Do you think she died of cold or was it of love, or of loneliness, or was it the curse that had befallen her?
> What do you make of all this?

Some discussion about what they have heard will follow led by the teacher out of role:

> Do you believe the old woman's story?
> Do you think that the old woman believed the story herself?
> How do you think that she got her information?
> With whom do you think she sympathised?
> What was her attitude to The Lady and Sir Lancelot?

• Extra option

The teacher can tell the class that the story includes many extracts from the poem. She reads the narrative again (or for the first time) and the children should clap their hands when they think they have heard phrases which they guess may have come from the poem. Teacher may wish to indicate with a gesture when the quotations appear, letting the children know when they are right.

Teachers may choose to read the whole poem to the children now that they know the plot and have heard the style of the language.

• Listening and understanding

The purpose of this activity is to give the children the plot without the risk of putting some of them off by reading the whole poem. Some more able children may also read the whole poem for themselves. Many classes will enjoy hearing the poem read aloud by the teacher or on tape now that they have been led carefully into the poem through this storytelling process.

The story has been written specifically to include many phrases from the poem. It is important that these are included because they then become familiar expressions. Having met them in the context of a more familiar and informal style, they will seem less daunting when met in the context of Tennyson's poem.

> To listen, understand and respond appropriately to others, pupils should be taught to identify the gist of an account or key points in a discussion and evaluate what they hear ... ask relevant questions to clarify, extend and follow up ideas. (DfEE/QCA, 2000: 50)

Activity (9)   Group formal readings (*Choral readings*)

Re-arrange the class into five groups. Part IV of the poem contains six verses. Each group is given one verse, excluding the last verse that they already know.

Each group must discuss and prepare a formal reading of their verse. They will stand in a line to read it. They should consider some or all of the following questions:

> Which lines should be louder/softer than others?
> Which words or phrases need to be stressed?
> When should there be many voices and when just a single voice?
> Would any gestures help convey meaning through the reading?
> Where should there be moments of silence, pauses between words or lines?
> Are there any examples of figurative language?
> What is the effect of repetition?
> Is there any significance in the sentence structure?

Each group performs their verse in the order of the poem, and the teacher reads the final familiar verse.

With some classes or groups within classes, it may be appropriate to give them larger sections to work on in this way.

Activity (10)   Playing with genre *(Small group story telling with images)*

Discuss genres such as horror, romance, mock horror, science fiction, sitcom, and detective/crime thrillers. The following questions may all be discussed with the class as a whole or a list of features of one genre such as horror could be constructed with the class as an example. Groups could discuss and produce lists of features of the other genres in the list.

> What do we expect in horror stories?
> What about mock horror? (e.g. *Dracula, Dead and Loving It*)
> What kind of characters do we find in crime thrillers/films/television?
> What do we expect of romances and science fiction stories?
> What sorts of things do we expect to find in comedy?

Groups of four or five are allocated a particular genre. They must deliver the following verse in the given genre. A romance will need an exaggerated dreamy expression, a horror genre will need looks of shock and surprise as well as suspense conveyed through pace and timing of delivery. Detective characters may be like well known media figures such as Columbo. The genre of comedy may include slapstick humour. The groups read the lines accompanied by action. Some groups may wish to have one reader. Others may decide to share out the lines as they engage in the action.

> She left the web, she left the loom
> She made three paces through the room,
> She saw the water lily bloom
> She saw the helmet and the plume,
> She looked down to Camelot.
> Out flew the web and floated wide;
> The mirror cracked from side to side;
> 'The curse is come upon me,' cried
> The Lady of Shalott.

- Genre discussion

This preparatory activity draws on children's knowledge and prior experience of a range of genres. The discussion generates a shared understanding of a variety of genres providing a platform of knowledge from which to move forward through practical exploration. Children often discover that they are already familiar with a range of *generic signifiers*, knowing the characteristics of the genre almost instinctively from their experience of reading and the media. They know for example that horrors often take place in large rambling buildings, at night, often in storms, and they can recognise the type of music associated with the genre. Once they have understood that a range of signifiers or features can be listed for one genre, they can quickly identify features for others:

> Pupils should be taught to use their knowledge of other texts they have read. (These texts can include comics, films, ballads, fairy tales or television programmes). (DfEE/QCA, 2000: 52)

- Genres in action

The verse used in this activity is perhaps the most exciting, with repetition, strong rhyme and direct speech.

This is a fun activity, which will lead to a close familiarity with the verse. At the same time, the consideration of other genres and the juxtaposition of these with Tennyson's lines invite a clearer understanding of the genre of *The Lady of Shalott*.

Activity (11) Narrative gap: the curse *(Small group playmaking)*

Groups of about five discuss how and why they think the curse may have been put on the Lady of Shalott in the first place. They should remember the key elements of walls, magic web, and mirror. They need to keep the feel of the poem's landscape and era. Once they have agreed upon their story of the curse they can do one of the following tasks:

> present their story with accompanying images sculpted as in activity (2);
> tell their story as a choral speaking presentation as in activity (8);
> enact their story.

- Inference and deduction

To fill the gap in the narrative children draw on their knowledge and understanding of this poetic text as well as on their previous experience of other texts such as fairy tales. Many familiar stories such as *Sleeping Beauty* and *Rumplestiltskin* include curses within their plot structure. Children draw on these and shape new curses to this particular context using their under-standing of the poem as a whole:

Pupils should be taught to:

a   use inference and deduction;
b   look for meaning beyond the literal;
c   make connections between different parts of text. (DfEE/QCA, 2000: 53)

Tennyson's poem and the range of activities described generate a wealth of additional and enriching possibilities. Teachers may find that any one of these activities yields ideas for further written, reading, oral or ICT learning opportunities. The notes below should give a sense of how far-reaching the tasks can be when stimulated by the drama activities based on the poem.

Additional activities

Individual written activity
Write individual stories which account for the possible origins of the curse in this poem.

Individual drawing and extract selection activity
Draw a story-board to depict the narrative of the poem, selecting one line from the poem as a caption for each board.

Oral pair activity
In pairs prepare a conversation that could have occurred between two gossips who live near the four grey towers, after they have heard about the woman's death.

Individual written activity
After activity (8) children can be given the list of quotations used in the narrative. They imagine that they are also people who were living in Camelot last year. Children individually write diary entries recounting the events from the point of view of someone else from Camelot – whoever the children wish to be! For example, a reaper or a boatman. They can be cynical, frightened, spiritual or melodramatic, but they must include all (or some) of the quotations provided in the list.

ICT opportunity

Images of Pre-Raphaelite paintings can be downloaded from the internet. There are many sites with the paintings of William John Waterhouse and William Holman Hunt. Examples include: www.nouveaunet.com and www. pre-raphaelites.com. Children can select particular paintings of *The Lady of Shalott* and decide which lines of the poem most closely relate to them.

Another exciting ICT opportunity is to photograph with a digital camera some of the sculpture made in the drama activities. Once on screen children can add sounds which would go with the images. These could include lines from the poem, perhaps sung, whispered etc. The images from the sculptures can also be manipulated on screen to heighten the effects.

On reflection

Classic texts may sometimes seem unapproachable to teachers as well as children. It is important that teaching materials are available which help teachers to feel confident and enthusiastic about giving the children interesting, challenging and different ways of exploring texts which at first appear difficult or outside their range of experience and everyday discourse.

Included in the References are books specifically about the teaching of drama for those who are keen to see other ways of using drama to enhance children's learning experiences not only for teaching classic poetry, but for improving specific writing and reading skills. This applies especially to the higher order reading skills of detailed reading and the probing of texts for meaning between and beyond the lines, as demonstrated in the lesson plan. The outcomes of dramatic activity are many and varied. They may be written, such as a poem, newspaper report, diary entry, character study or play script, but they do not have to be written. The outcome may be discussion, or drawings, diagrams, a physical and symbolic image, an agreed statement, a video-tape or a sound effects audio tape. The high level of motivation generated through dramatic activity often enables children to reach the higher level of outcome, whatever its nature.

Many drama activities, such as those detailed in this chapter, can of course be used within the structure of the literacy hour. Most of the activities can be carried out within the first fifteen minutes of the hour during the shared text work. Here the drama activity becomes the shared text, usually an oral text, which is constructed either by the whole class or by groups of children, performed and then discussed. In this instance, the lesson plan will be covered over a series of literacy hour sessions. Boulton (2000) provided an example of how an extended drama divided up into purposeful sections can offer the full range of literacy requirements over the course of a week.

Learning occurs in different ways for different children. One child's possibilities for achieving excellence in English may initially appear to be through individual reading and writing work. However, it is likely that the child will discover other and perhaps unexpected insights and skills through interactive and collaborative work. This could come through working in dramatic form. Another child may find individual reading and writing tasks limiting and failing to provide adequate motivation. They may serve only to inhibit the child's chances of achieving excellence in English. Having experienced practical interactive activities such as those they will encounter in the drama described above, the standard of such a child's writing is likely to improve (Neelands, 1993; Boshell, 2000). It is a personal and often emotional commitment to the practical work that generates a motive or desire to write. An obvious advantage of using drama for teaching English is that most children really enjoy doing it. Having got over the issue of motivation, a teacher can quickly take the children into the imagined contexts and build on their enthusiasm. Perhaps, therefore to maximise every child's opportunity to achieve excellence in English, teachers must employ a wide range of teaching strategies including dramatic form. Through using drama teachers can give fictional reasons for children to look more deeply into a text, achieve a broader understanding and develop critical insight.

As teachers we know when we have achieved excellence in our teaching. There are clear indicators; the children are motivated and committed to the work, and as a result, they enjoy their learning. Under these conditions, children rise to new challenges. Drama introduces active engagement with fiction, which automatically brings a pleasure dimension to the tasks set. It draws upon children's natural ability to play and pretend whilst exploiting their experiences of the media such as television and computer games. If the children are enjoying themselves, the teachers will enjoy themselves, too, but more significantly, they can introduce higher levels of learning and push the children to achieve their maximum potential.

4. 'Great Expectations by Charles Dickens, Wicked!' Teaching Classic Literature in Year 6

Kate Hirom

The words in the title of this chapter were spoken by my 10-year-old niece when I jokingly presented her with my battered hardback copy of *Great Expectations* in place of the Michael Morpurgo book that I had really bought her as a present. Her unexpectedly enthusiastic response caused the joke to backfire. 'We've been doing this in school. It's a brilliant book', she went on to say. 'We watched the video.'

This had been her first experience of an adult text and her first experience of the classics. Aided by the black and white 1947 David Lean film version it had evidently been a positive one. It cannot be said that subsequently *Great Expectations* has replaced my niece's preferred independent reading though she was very eager to read the first chapter again with me, reading in parts, alternating so that each had a chance to be the convict. Cara is a keen reader though she describes herself as a slow reader. Like everyone else she enjoys *Harry Potter*, but she has taken some time to persevere through the first two volumes, interspersed with her real enthusiasms, anything by Jacqueline Wilson and the next volume in the *Stacey and Friends* series. It may be some while before she can pursue independently a pre-twentieth century novel of this length and complexity; nevertheless, clearly, she has been given an introduction that will dispose her to associate the work of Dickens with pleasure. Intrigued to know how this enthusiasm had been inspired I contacted her teacher, Jeff Evans. Examples from the scheme of work developed by his colleague Gina Luckhurst are included in this chapter.

In another lesson in a different school the class had been reading *Tom's Midnight Garden*. The lesson took place in the summer of 1998 in the first year of the National Literacy Strategy. In this particular lesson the teacher read the penultimate chapter to the class. He then went on to produce a battered bag, out of which he drew several mysterious parcels of different shapes and sizes. These, he said, had been found in the old house. Each of the parcels was unwrapped and a discussion ensued as to whom they could belong. A particular focus of the class's attention was the largest and most bulky of the packages. 'Hattie's skates, Hattie's skates' was the excited murmur. Indeed, so it proved to be. One little girl, forgetting momentarily that this was a lesson in a classroom, asked 'are they really Hattie's skates?' so powerful was the momentary 'suspension of disbelief' which is the essential ingredient of entering into what Tolkein called the 'secondary world' of the novel. After some brief discussion about the significance of the skates and how they happened to be there the lesson moved on to word level work and a study of adverbs. I was reminded of the words on the clock in the book when Tom's sojourn in his other world was coming to an end, 'Time no longer!' Under the imperative of the literacy hour clock we hurried on.

What interests me about these two anecdotes is the excitement generated in children by the study of literature. In the one case I had been privileged to be part of a reading group in which through good reading, a little harmless deception and an imaginative use of props, the teacher had managed to inject a palpable sense of awe and wonder into the classroom quite in keeping with the fantasy novel being studied. In the other case a spontaneous recall of 'a rich experience of more challenging texts' (DfEE, 1998), one of the primary aims of 'shared reading' within the literacy strategy, had been stimulated by a focused study. Key factors in its success had been:

- immersion in the historical context of *Great Expectations;*
- an introduction to other works of the author;
- judicious selection of a sequence of narrative extracts;
- comparison with a film version.

I wish to use both of these anecdotes to explore the notion of excellence in the teaching of literature at Key Stage 2. Both happen to relate to the teaching of 'classics', the one an adult Victorian text and the other a book written for children in the 1950s which involves a time switch to the Victorian age.

What are classics?

The chapter is entitled 'classic literature' because the term is used within the National Literacy Strategy and it is, after all, a term in common parlance. In the context of teaching in schools it may be seen as part of a 'cultural heritage' model of English teaching, which 'emphasises the responsibility of schools to lead children to an appreciation of those works of literature that have been widely regarded as amongst the finest in the language' (Cox, 1995).

According to Watson (1991) a group of 10-year-olds provided the definition, 'Books written by dead people.' He suggested that 'the word "classic" in its many contexts almost always suggests an excellence surviving from a past age' and went on to say 'such a book does not simply endure like a fossil in a glass case, but is constantly re-made and improvised upon so that its qualities and its appeal are transformed and revealed to new generations of readers'.

Classics, he submitted, are part of our national vocabulary. 'The great children's classics are those books our national consciousness cannot leave alone.' As Powling (1991) suggested, 'To survive as a classic, a book must maintain its integrity through infinite variation' which, in order to meet the interests of a technological age will include not only dramatisations and different print formats but film adaptations including animation. Watson (1991: 4) went on to identify a feature he believed to be an essential ingredient of a children's classic.

> Among the thousands of books written for children, there appears now and again one which, through some mysterious alchemy, the author has transformed into a metaphor expressing the ways in which children and adults love one another.

It expresses an intimacy between adult and child reader. His choices are interesting. John Burningham's *Granpa* is in his list of classics whereas C.S. Lewis's *Narnia* books are not because 'despite his undoubted brilliance as a story maker, Lewis' conception of children is distant and narrow'. Eccleshare (2001: 3) defined children's classics as 'the books that have lasted, building bridges between generations, tapping into the constants of childhood and of parent/child relationships'.

There are many who would contest these universal constants and the unquestioned consensus about what is the finest and the best. Many would see the notion of 'national consciousness' as a political contrivance that poses an illusory consensus by privileging dominant cultural values over the greater diversity of people's real, lived experiences. They may suggest that, in many cases, the survival of certain texts has more to do with their potential to be reproduced as lavishly costumed period dramas aimed at the American market, than with their intrinsic literary merits. It is also the case that endurance of the classics is a manifestation of the conservative nature of the canon of literature prescribed for study in universities and colleges for many years and that a narrow view of what constitutes 'worthy reading' for children and young adults has influenced the choice of books bought by adults for children. For example Eccleshare (2001) made the valid point that many of the parents who urge their children to purchase *Treasure Island* in bookshops have never actually read it, although they think they have so ubiquitous are the references to Long John Silver, 'pieces of eight' and Blind Pugh. The definition has been extended further by the marketing of a variety of texts by publishers as 'modern classics' including relatively recent titles such as *Carrie's War* by Nina Bawden largely on the grounds of sales figures over a period of time. What is included as a children's classic and what is left out is of interest. Although Enid Blyton is the most published author of modern times and still figures prominently on lists of children's favourites she is rarely included in lists of recommended texts.

Fisher (1991) quoted Kenneth Graham's description of his own child's reading. 'What the Boy chiefly dabbled in was natural history and fairy tales, and he just took them as they came in a sandwichy sort of way.' She saw this as a sensible approach. 'The classics should be tossed to children as interesting food to be sampled not virtuously but as sandwiches whose fillings might surprise them' (28). It is essential that 'classics' are not viewed with reverence as the gold standard of children's reading but are judged on their own terms for their ability to engage young readers. Both in the National Curriculum and the National Literacy Strategy the term 'long-established' is used with regard to literature written specifically for children. Whilst all such labels as 'significant', 'long established' and 'classic' are open to interpretation this bears fewer hierarchical overtones. It is important to recognise that a literary text is not 'excellent' because of its label, but because its excellence has been validated by readers.

In school as well as at home children should encounter child characters in a variety of settings, a variety of situations, and different historical times. Excellence in the teaching of literature is achieved not by the text alone but by the synergy of text, teacher and children. The process must not be one way. Children must be given the opportunity to introduce texts that they consider excellent. Indeed, some of my most successful classroom texts have been adopted on the recommendation of children. However, there are many texts that children may not discover for themselves and teachers have the responsibility of extending children's reading experiences in areas where they would not, otherwise, have the confidence to go. It is also important to recognise that teachers may have some part to play in establishing the classics of the future which should represent a wider diversity of cultural experiences and traditions than is evident in our present notions of the 'classic'.

Excellent teaching of literature opens up new worlds, encourages participation, and intrigues and delights children with the power of words, and motivates them with the desire for more.

The pleasure in the text

Writing just before the introduction of the literacy strategy Hynds (1998: 11) expressed some anxiety that:

> with this over-mechanical programme concentrating as it does mainly on the assumed hierarchical skills of literacy, children are going to be hard put in school to read for pleasure and entertainment, and that kind of self-fulfilment which committed and involved readers regularly experience. Texts in the project are invariably chosen for 'study' and for 'focused work', not for enjoyment.

This is a well justified fear according to Frater's (2000: 110) reflections on surveys of literacy hour lessons in thirty-two primary schools:

> No novels were seen in use in either of the KS2 surveys. Where texts were in evidence they were usually short pieces or extracts and they were read, not for their pleasure or values as literature, but for their illustrative force on a point of grammar or language knowledge.

Reading is a public as well as a private process: public in that writers use, and consciously divert from, culturally defined generic conventions in language and structure; private in that no two readers will react to a text in precisely the same way. Different critical approaches tend to privilege one approach or the other though most will agree that the meaning of a text resides in the negotiation between what is in the text and what the reader brings to it. The way in which literature is taught in the classroom will, as with most pedagogy, depend on the balance between the teacher's values and the prevailing ideology of the time. During the 1990s the writings of Benton and Fox (1985) were influential in advocating an approach based on a theory of reader response. The emphasis fell upon teaching the class novel in a way that simulates, stimulates and supports the sort of reading behaviour used by the committed and engaged individual reader – picturing, anticipating and retrospecting, interacting and evaluating. The teacher's role was to be sensitive to the children's social involvement with the writer and to their imaginative involvement with the world of the text, asking children very tentatively to step outside and evaluate. 'What do you feel about the way the story is being told?' Activities were designed to facilitate these different reading processes.

The literacy strategy model begins with the text as a cultural product and looks at how it works largely independently of the reader's response. Termly objectives tend to begin with words such as 'analyse', 'identify', 'classify', 'compare' and 'evaluate' and the approach is generally atomistic rather than holistic. The analogy is often drawn between this sort of detailed criticism and the dissection of a butterfly, with the clear implication that after we have pulled apart the wings we are left with the cold and lifeless parts of something once vibrant and colourful. However, as the work of Heath (1983) showed, it cannot be assumed that all children approach fictional narrative with a shared understanding of what it is, how it works, or what it is supposed to do. Benton and Fox (1985) did include sections in their text which acknowledged that there are times when engagement is clearly not happening. Making children aware of the different ways in which writers manipulate the different conventions (for example in story openings, endings) can enable inexperienced readers to understand the pattern or schema, to draw threads together to discern emerging themes and lead to speedier reading and greater private enjoyment. It is also the case that some more difficult texts such as *Great Expectations* require more 'study' than texts that are more easily accessible.

Warlow (1977), still a goldmine for reflections and critical readings on the relationship between writers and readers of children's fiction, concluded that critical reading and the sort of imaginative involvement that comes from being absorbed in a book are distinct kinds of reading but not necessarily antithetical. He quoted Squire's (1964: 91) conclusion to a study of adolescent reading and critical response. 'The two types of reading seem to reinforce one another with readers who are emotionally involved forming more literary judgements even though the responses occur at different times'. The critical would seem to operate after the imaginative engagement.

The literacy strategy provides rich opportunities for the reading of a wide and mixed diet of different kinds of literature and has been received enthusiastically by many teachers as a result. However there does seem to be a lack of appreciation that unlike other genres, for example instructional texts, the social function of literary texts is above all to provide understanding through pleasure. Instructional texts do not require people to *feel*, merely to understand. Comprehension of a fictional text is not only an intellectual activity. Commitment and involvement are central to the modelling of experienced reading, and the affective response of teacher and children must not be viewed as inferior to the analytical. It is, therefore, as important that the teacher spends as much time on the creation of an exciting communal experience as upon technical features of style or structure, if our vision is to extend beyond immediate assessment objectives to the future reading life of the child. There is some anecdotal evidence from schools in my locality that, whilst SATs scores in reading have improved, the volume of reading has actually gone down.

Graham (1999) reporting on an action research project in Croydon aiming to improve children's reading at Key Stage 2 in 1995 emphasised the importance of teachers sharing their enthusiasm for books. After participants had reviewed different texts for possible use in the classroom: 'Project teachers began to realise that the texts they selected to take back to school were those which had been enthusiastically introduced in the book review sessions by colleagues' (107). Project teachers concentrated on 'performance reading aloud' which was much appreciated by pupils in the project classes.

> 'She acted as if she was really in the story, like when they shouted in the story, she shouted.' (Year 3 pupil)

Children were given the opportunity to practise performance reading for themselves, sometimes re-visiting passages shared as a class, as Graham put it 'practising the tunes' of the language. Although this is a feature of Key Stage 1 reading teachers felt that some of their pupils, particularly boys, had somehow missed this along the way. The teachers in the project schools showed their own affective enjoyment by laughing at the funny bits, looking scared at the frightening parts and in sad parts sometimes having eyes full of tears. They built up a collaborative atmosphere in classrooms, admitting in group readings that they also needed to rehearse before reading aloud.

According to one pupil good teachers of reading 'make you feel confident not embarrassed … and make it fun' (113).

Many years before the introduction of the literacy strategy framework, Winograd and Johnson (1987: 226) wrote:

> We are concerned that the pressures of accountability may cause teachers to focus on reading as if the transfer of information were the only concern and thereby ignore reading as a way of developing relationships with children and relationships as a way of developing children's reading. We feel strongly that an essential aspect of learning to read is the rapport that develops when teachers take the time to share the pleasures of reading with their students.

This engagement can only really be built up by extended immersion in a complete text. Text extracts have their place to enable comparison of, for example, different story openings or to provide tasters of different works by the same author or to stimulate interest in and awareness of a wide range of texts. (Many parents relate that their children have come home eager to look for books in the library as a result of an intriguing introduction to a literary text). A teacher in Graham's study (1999: 107) said: 'I read exciting snippets from a different book every few days. The book is then placed in the library, where it is soon snapped up to be read.' Where an extract has been used as the focus of close study the children should, at the very least, see that it comes from a real book and that they should know something about what it has to offer.

Arguing for the use of the novel as opposed to the fragmented textual experience of reading schemes as the best way of developing children's higher order reading skills Currie (1997) described the importance of the novel in the construction of schemata as a way of structuring knowledge. In other words information is not stored as a series of random items but as linked events and information gained from experience or from within a text. Schemata are used in the interpretation process in various ways for example in inference. The thematic nature of the novel, building chapter by chapter on what has gone before, enables children to develop a growing body of knowledge in which to integrate new information and from which to make predictions and inferences. There is no need to set up each time new schemata for settings and characters. 'To achieve similar effects using disconnected texts (as is common with most reading schemes) the teacher would have to prepare children by stimulating the relevant schemata for each new passage' (Currie, 1997: 14).

What is word level work? What does it mean?

One of the saddest aspects of observations of student literacy hour lessons is to observe a literary text, either in 'shared' or 'guided' reading being used as a source of a search for prefixes or suffixes, or even for the writer's use of adjectives and adverbs with no discussion of the force of the particular lexical choice. Children need to have an awareness that the experienced writer uses the grammar and vocabulary of the language as a toolkit from which he or she selects the best nuts and bolts for the job in hand. The fact that writers use adjectives and adverbs is of less interest than *which* adverbs and adjectives have been chosen and for what purpose. The teacher is not only modelling his or her own response to the themes and content of the narrative but also to the language. Children can only use literary texts as models for their own writing if language has been internalised and embedded in their own linguistic repertoires. In order to do this they must have felt the force of the language for themselves. Language is a structured system but it is also fluid, ambiguous and endlessly changing. Good writing embodies a range of linguistic choices. There are occasions in the novel when its purpose is functional and low key. At other times it should hit you with surprise, delight or a sense of its perfect aptness.

Children are reportedly impatient of long descriptive passages in books of their own choosing. One of the attractions of Enid Blyton's books for children is in their stock phrases that do not interrupt the ongoing thrust of the plot by drawing attention to themselves. Descriptions are a kind of short-hand that signal to the reader, 'cornflower blue' means 'sea'. No need to dwell on that. Move on. Many young children, however, love new and com-plicated words. Teachers need to build on this and to express their own enjoyment of words; to savour and reflect on them; to dwell on their sounds and strangeness, explore what they *might* mean, investigate their etymology, ask children which words they like and why, encourage them to collect good words from the texts they encounter. In addition, part of the purpose of shared reading is to explore texts using what one teacher in the DfEE literacy strategy video referred to as 'premiership words' – words that really count.

Teaching Dickens

In discussing the teaching of classic texts in Key Stage 2 I aim to refer back to the aspects of good practice identified previously, drawing examples from this material. However, first, it is necessary to justify the teaching of an adult Victorian novel to Year 6 children in the primary school when there are now so many accessible children's texts which may be seen as closer to their interests, experience and independent reading levels. In a curriculum in which the central cause for celebration is the opportunity to engage with a diversity of different literature it is important that children can develop a sense of the historical development of language and literature as well as the broader definitions of cultural experience. Many of my undergraduate students, never having read a Victorian novel previously pronounce them 'hard to get into' and often say: 'I didn't really think that I was going to enjoy it.' Children come to the text with fewer prejudices. The introduction of the Victorian novel in Year 6 in conjunction with cross-curricular work on history provides children with the opportunity to locate the production of the novel within its historical period. Gina Luckhurst's scheme was originally taught in Year 7 when the school was a middle school and has since been adapted to meet the classics objectives of the literacy strategy framework. In the mixed ability Year 6 class the introduction to Dickens is conducted in careful stages: initially with short comprehension passages taken from *A Christmas Carol* and *Oliver Twist*. This is intended to get the children gradually into Dickens' style and whilst the questions are differentiated the language is Dickens' own. Thereafter the more extended work on *Great Expectations* is undifferentiated but Jeff Evans reported that the lower achieving children did not experience difficulty in engaging with the text. Of course, either of the other texts could make a self-contained unit of work and have the advantage in that many children would be familiar with the stories from the film versions. As the contemporary children's writer Morpurgo states in his introduction to the Collins abridged version of *Oliver Twist*:

> Dickens' triumph is to have written a story so powerful, so universal, so true, that we can learn as much from it now as his readers did in his lifetime … All through it we long to call out to him [Oliver], to warn him, to protect him, hold his hand, hope he'll come through.

However as Moss (1997) warned it is important that any abridgement does not unnecessarily replace the richness of Dickens' own language with language rendered lifeless in the name of accessibility. An abridged version to be preferred for teachers and pupils is the Puffin Classics series which retains the original language.

It is a feature of the literacy strategy that texts previously taught at secondary level have been adapted to the learning level of children at the top of Key Stage 2 and to many teachers the children's capabilities have proved a revelation. It is, however, vitally important that children come away from the study of any text with the feeling that it was 'wicked' rather than a feat of endurance.

Why Dickens?

Of all the Victorian novelists Dickens stands out as particularly appropriate for use in the classroom for the following reasons listed randomly:

- the strong, clearly delineated characters often associated with easily memorable 'catch phrases';
- the dramatic dialogue, which is fun to read aloud;
- his depiction of social inequality and the moral questions raised;
- the humorous interludes and character portrayal as well as dramatic set pieces;
- his style, sometimes rather dense for children to grasp, but at other times joyously 'over the top';
- the importance of setting and his ability to create atmosphere;
- the existence of a number of video versions to compare with the text;
- video versions help children visualise the settings;
- the opportunity for cross curricular work on the Victorians;
- his ability to understand the frustrations and vulnerability of children (despite the retrospective view of some of his novels);
- his influence on modern writers, notably Roald Dahl whose grotesque characters would provide an interesting comparison.

Many schools include some Dickens within their schemes of work, often using single de-contextualised extracts in published schemes, favourites being the character portrayal of Miss Havisham from *Great Expectations* or school scenes from *Nicholas Nickleby* or *David Copperfield*. The advantage of a Dickens' unit rather than isolated extracts is that children need time to 'get into' the world of the novels as well as the unfamiliar language. Pupils who have also encountered workhouses, the treadmill, and the Poor Laws (as mentioned in chapter one of *A Christmas Carol*) in history lessons will have additional knowledge to bring to the text thus developing and drawing from rich schemata. Additional sources of information in relation to the workhouse and child labour can be found on the internet and in local historical documents. A useful link between literacy and history is provided by the use of such resources as the Victorian pack from the Nicholas Roberts Publications (1998). This provides for a range of writing and comprehension tasks based on an extract from *David Copperfield*, contemporary letters and newspaper reports. Particularly useful are those glossy, coloured reproductions of paintings depicting the urban poor, workhouses and Florence Nightingale in the Crimean field hospitals. Materials are differentiated and provide supportive writing frames for a variety of genres.

Of course *A Christmas Carol* is celebrated for its cheerful depiction of the Victorian Christmas in which Dickens was influential in his own day for setting the style. Children will enjoy sharing the remark of the little costermonger's girl on the death of Dickens in 1870, 'Mr Dickens dead? Then will Father Christmas die too?'

A Christmas Carol

A good starting point for an entry into Dickens' style is the description of Scrooge.

> Oh! But he was a tight-fisted hand at the grindstone, Scrooge! A squeezing, wrenching, grasping, clutching, covetous old sinner! Hard and sharp as a flint, from which no steel had ever struck out a generous fire; secret, and self-contained, and solitary as an oyster. The cold within him froze his old features, nipped his pointed nose, shrivelled his cheek, stiffened his gait; made his eyes red, his thin lips blue; and spoke out shrewdly in his grating voice. A frosty rime was on his head, and on his eyebrows, and on his wiry chin. He carried his low temperature always about with him; he iced his coffee in the dog-days, and didn't thaw it one degree at Christmas.

The rhythm of the language cries out for 'performance reading aloud'. The words should be savoured and relished before any explanation of archaic vocabulary items such as 'covetous', 'rime', 'gait' and 'dog-days'.

Of course, the origins and meaning of the words are also of interest, for example 'dog-days' to describe the hottest period of the year (from the Roman belief that the rising of the dog star added to the heat of the sun). There are also grammatical features of interest – the listing of the present participles 'squeezing' 'wrenching', 'grasping', 'clutching' as noun qualifiers; the ellipsis of 'he was' in the second and third sentences but mainly it is the musicality of the words that we would want to appreciate first.

A class in which I taught this novel was asked what they remembered of the description of Scrooge in a subsequent lesson and I was delighted by the response of a pupil with special needs who rarely contributed an answer. 'He was as solitary as an oyster, Miss' said with a horribly screwed up face. The simile had captured her imagination but what an odd, though surprisingly apt, simile it is! A teacher would want to explore this with a class. The language of Dickens is endlessly inventive and surprising, some of it drawn from sayings in his own day and some of it his own. There are few people who are not familiar with 'bah humbug' and another favourite and memorable quotation for children is that of Marley's ghost: 'I wear the chain I forged in life. I made it link by link and yard by yard.'

Another interesting passage for close analysis and the one chosen in Gina Luckhurst's scheme is the description of Christmas activities and Christmas food. The vision of the second apparition of the shops overflowing with seasonal foods: 'round pot-bellied baskets of chestnuts' 'candied fruits so caked and spotted with molten sugar', 'figs … moist and pulpy' assails the senses and, whilst we would not wish our pupils to write in this overloaded way always, it provides an excellent model for creative writing and word level work as would the Cratchits' Christmas meal. Dickens' own belief in the importance of family life is well represented in the portrait of the Cratchits. It is an interesting biographical note that he himself had ten children and it is worthwhile reflecting on what being a mother often meant in those days. That Dickens himself was not always the most supportive husband is another aspect to this famous advocate of public social reform.

A Christmas Carol is also interesting for the way in which it was produced. Written hastily when the family were in need of quick money, the novel seems to have been hugely enjoyed by Dickens himself. The publication was also paid for out of his own pocket and priced so that it was affordable for many. The fact that pirate copies undermined his profits provides an interesting parallel with the media industry today. When teaching a historical text it is important to provide children with opportunities to draw parallels and contrasts with their own experience.

A Christmas Carol is a useful medium through which children can reflect upon differences between times past and times present. An interesting group activity is to ask children to imagine that the Ghost of Christmas Future shows Scrooge images from 2001. What scenes would they select and what is likely to surprise Scrooge most? Ask them to include some bad scenes from present day life as well as the good. The exercise is interesting in what it reveals about children's perceptions of the world around them and what they consider to be of cultural significance.

A different exercise in comparative values can be provided by consideration of Dickens as a cultural commodity widely marketed in different forms throughout the world. In many countries children read or see versions of the works of Dickens and with no experience to refer to they imagine that they represent a true depiction of Britain today. It is a more sophisticated task, but not too difficult for some children, to invite them to describe the impression of British life that an outsider might derive from the works of Dickens. Children can begin to appreciate the dangers of defining other cultures from their representation in fiction.

Great Expectations

Great Expectations may seem a surprising choice in view of its length, the complexity of its plot and the adult themes of disappointment, loss and corruption. However the novel is easily divided into phases and the childhood scenes are accessible. The availability of the black and white David Lean version of the text is an added bonus. Whilst there are several film versions it is, in my opinion, the most atmospheric. The opening sequences in the churchyard and the scenes depicting the bleak marshland, with the gibbet against the skyline provide an instant dramatic impact and are sympathetic to the dark atmosphere of the text. In Gina Luckhurst's scheme the printed text of chapter one is read first, though some teachers might prefer to use the film narrative first. The order of texts serves different functions. In the printed text first version the children have built up their own pictures of the character and the scene and, with the support of some prompting questions, can be more attuned to the details they expect to see in the moving image version based on their understanding of the text. However chapter one can be rather confusing in its entirety. The opening paragraphs where the naïve child narrator reflects upon the appearance of his dead parents and brothers and sisters based on the position of the tombstones and the shape of the lettering on the inscriptions is very subtly humorous and needs some explanation after which the humour can be lost. That Pip has lost many of his little brothers and sisters, and his parents makes an interesting historical discussion about the differences in life expectancy, and increases the pathos.

The encounter between Pip and the convict is quite dramatic enough to engage children immediately and teachers may choose to begin there leaving the tombstones to be recovered visually in the video. The vigorous dialogue invites 'performance reading'. The children should be asked to share their mental pictures of the central characters and the setting and to compare them later with what they have seen. As Oldham (1999) emphasised it is important that children know that the film they are watching is someone's interpretation and need not be theirs. Also of interest is the way in which the first person perspective of the written text, descriptions of thoughts and feelings, are translated into the camera angle of the moving image version. Children do not need to use any particular technical language though 'close-up' will be a part of many children's vocabulary. They might like to talk about the way in which Pip's description of being turned upside down by the convict is represented on the screen.

Showing the video first provides an instant way in to the text, sets the mood and tone, and can aid comprehension of its difficult aspects. In Oldham's discussion of a pilot project undertaken by The Centre for Research on Literacy and the Media, using *Oliver Twist* with a Key Stage 3 class, she found that the confidence in the narrative provided by the video aided skimming and scanning for key words. In Gina Luckhurst's scheme the watching of the video of chapter one is followed by a comprehension focusing on word level work in chapter two and a written prediction on the end of the chapter, the raid on the pantry. The children then watch the video and discuss the image of the winking hare, the symbol of Pip's guilt; in his mind in the novel, but a physical reality in the film.

Parker (1999: 30) emphasised the knowledge about narrative that children bring with them to school from their pre-print encounters with moving image literacy. 'Bringing this into the classroom bridges the gap between out-of-school enculturated language and literacy practice, and what, by comparison, can seem to be a stilted and decontextualised schooled literacy.' Moving image versions can be found in many of the adult and children's classics. The film education pack *Film and Literacy Pack: part 1* uses video clips from *James and the Giant Peach* and *The Railway Children* to explore the narrative point of view. With a long and complex text such as *Great Expectations*, where it is not possible or desirable to read the text as a whole, the use of video clips can provide narrative links between chapters to be read as well as narrative closure. As Benton and Fox (1985) suggested, the sense of anticipation is an important driving force in any reading and children should not be left with the sense of an incomplete text. How much of the print text is actually read will depend on the time available. I would certainly want to include chapter eight which narrates Pip's first visit to Satis House and his first encounter with Miss Havisham and Estella. The chapter includes the character portrayal of Miss Havisham often singled out for de-contextualised analysis. It is also, however, central to the character development of the adult narrator in that it is here that he first develops his dissatisfaction with his home, his social position and consequently his whole being.

> 'He calls the knaves, Jacks, this boy!' said Estella with disdain before our first game was out. 'And what coarse hands he has and what coarse thick boots!'

> ... I set off on the four-mile walk to our forge; pondering all that I had seen, and deeply revolving that I was a common labouring boy; that my hands were coarse; that my boots were thick; that I had fallen into a despicable habit of calling knaves, Jacks; that I was much more ignorant than I had considered myself last night, and generally that I was in a low lived bad way.

This chapter, though strange, is perfectly accessible, and provides a possible link with pupil experiences (who has not at some time been 'shown up'?) as well as some discussion about attitudes to dialect and social class distinctions in Victorian England and today.

I would also include chapter thirty-nine where the convict Magwitch returns, revealing himself as Pip's benefactor.

The flexible literacy hour

Teachers may well object that this video watching is all very well but how does it fit into the structure of the literacy hour? In the school scheme described above, which was the subject of favourable comments by OFSTED, the Year 6 team adopts a flexible approach to the literacy hour so that the stage in the text determines whether the hour is used on one day for text work only and on another for word level work. A similar flexibility might be extended to the objectives for different terms.

Frater (2000: 109) concluded that in schools where literacy teaching was weakest:

> One of the clearest problems seemed to lie in the very closeness of [this] conscientious adherence to the provisions of the NLS. The least progress in embedding, as distinct from observing the requirements of the strategy, had been observed in those who had been anxious about or preoccupied by covering the termly content of the framework – leading to a highly literal interpretation.

In a resource-led scheme, objectives from the second term may well be delivered in the first if the text lends itself to it or vice versa. The most effective teachers of literacy in the study by Wray and Medwell (1998) were those who had identified their own values and taught with commitment and conviction. Teachers who love language and love books will make children interested in them too. They will be discerning and flexible in interpreting the structure of the literacy framework and imaginative and inventive in their teaching approaches. If teachers are to teach with conviction they must have the opportunity to explore their own beliefs and values. The most thought provoking of Frater's reflections on observations of the less encouraging aspects of the literacy strategy is that, 'many staff seemed ... wittingly or unwittingly – to have suppressed the love of language and literature that had first brought them into the profession' (109). The conflict between what they would like to do and what they perceive they 'ought to do' is reflected also in the anxious comments of trainees. A student had been studying *Alice in Wonderland* for her dissertation and was planning a cross-curricular 'Wonderland Week'. She had visited Christ Church, Oxford and had drawn together some fascinating insights on the possible influences of Carroll's work. She did not think she could use this with her class, however, 'because considering how texts are rooted in the writer's experience doesn't come in until Year 5 term 1. Likewise, I'd really love to do homophones with this class. There are so many examples in the book. But it's not one of our objectives for this term'.

When I asked Jeff Evans, 'Why Dickens?' it was clear that the impetus had really come from Gina Luckhurst's personal enthusiasm both for the novels of Dickens and for the film, an enthusiasm she had passed on to him and so to my niece. By using video versions of the text children were learning to employ two forms of what Scholes (1985) termed 'narrativity', or in other words the reader's contribution to the narrative. In the print medium, he suggested, the reader is involved much of the time in creating visual images and may, therefore, spend less time in the work of interpretation. In the film narrative, the viewer is given the images but must supply the interpretation of the images presented. He thus provides a theoretical explanation of the ways in which the use of film in the classroom may enhance comprehension. In addition, however, there is an growing recognition that communication in the twenty-first century is increasingly conveyed through visual images. Heath (2001) submitted that it is a fallacy to suggest that children automatically understand how to read pictures. She argued that beginning in childhood and continuing into adolescence children need to be taught how to see and that visual literacy should be included as an important part of what counts as literacy. To use video and printed texts alongside each other in the classroom are therefore complementary activities in the making of meaning from texts. The great film director Sergei Eisenstein in 1944 put forward the view that the film director D.W. Griffith actually learnt his technique of montage from Dickens. He asked the question:

> What were the novels of Dickens for his contemporaries, for his readers? There is one answer: they bore the same relation to them that the film bears to the same strata in our time.
>
> The secret lies in Dickens' (as well as the cinema's) extraordinary plasticity. The observation in the novels is extraordinary – as is their optical quality. The characters of Dickens are rounded with means as plastic and slightly exaggerated as are the screen heroes of today. The screen's heroes are engraved on the senses of the spectator with clearly visible traits; its villains are remembered by certain facial expressions, and all are saturated in the peculiar, slightly radiant gleam thrown over them by the screen.
>
> It is absolutely thus that Dickens draws his characters ... (cited in Mast and Cohen, 1974: 37)

Eisenstein described literature as, 'in the first and most important place: the art of viewing' both in the mind's eye and in the observation of the 'real' world. When children are engaged with Dickens they are discovering the way in which he 'read' the world of his time: what he noticed, how he saw it, what he wanted to say about it and how he transformed it into his own world, the world of the text, in his mind's eye. As Freire (1987) pointed out we begin reading the world long before we encounter print literacy. What we aim to do as teachers of literature is to enable children to use their experiences of literature of all kinds to read the world in new and challenging ways. For this to happen they will also have needed to have engaged the mind's eye.

I have endeavoured in this chapter to suggest that excellence in the teaching of literature goes far beyond the mining of text for grammatical terminology. Excellent teaching of literature will:

- acknowledge that the social purpose of literature is to provide pleasure;
- understand that 'comprehension' of a literary text involves an affective as well as an intellectual response;
- encourage the sharing of affective responses with both teachers and pupils;
- help to enable pupils to have opportunities to inhabit the world of the text as well as to stand outside and evaluate it;
- recognise that whilst critical evaluation and imaginative engagement are both important, imaginative engagement should come first;
- make discussion of books an exciting communal literary event, not just an opportunity to transmit information;
- explore different ways of creating a literary event which includes reading as performance; activities which share the element of play in literature including drama activities and use of video material;
- use moving image material to provide different ways of supporting children's understanding of written narrative as well as an understanding of visual narrative;
- enthuse children with a wide variety of books including introducing them to more complex texts that they may come to fully appreciate later;
- demonstrate genuine interest in language and provide multi-sensory ways in which children can appreciate the power of language;
- respect where children are but aim to take them further.

5. Curriculum Leadership: a beginner's guide

Kathy Caddy

This chapter represents a personal account of the organising and working out of an English co-ordinator's role. Although it should prove useful for teachers who are already 'in harness' as co-ordinators, it is put together mainly for those who have just begun such a role or have been co-ordinators for only a little while. Essentially, the intention is give readers (ambitious, budding co-ordinators!) ideas on how to plan, implement and develop their roles. To achieve this end, and to maximise impact, the chapter will address beginning co-ordinators directly, with the belief that even those with other roles may sooner or later take up such a co-ordinating position, or will benefit from realising what the position involves. English is so fundamental to everything children do, it inevitably has a high priority in schools (certainly, it should not be confined to the 'literacy hour', since there are so many other ways a teacher can make the subject vital and exciting). Over time, subject co-ordination becomes very much what the incumbent makes of it. Personally, I think it is much more adventurous to develop a role rather than just maintain it. The difficulty is finding time to do all the things anyone might wish to do.

Where do you start?

Let us begin at the beginning. It is your first week as English co-ordinator, where *do* you start? It is useful to settle securely into the job without too much delay and gain the respect of colleagues. Nevertheless, it is prudent to take one step at a time. Do not try to do too many things at once. Just become familiar with the role's scope first of all and pin down what is essential to it. I am going to suggest many ideas that could eventually become your responsibility, but remember I mean just that: *eventually*, your responsibility! The longer you teach, the easier the job becomes and the more straightforward it is to introduce ever richer and more experimental ideas into what is undertaken. I would not want to frighten anyone into assuming that all, or even half of the things I am going to suggest, are essential to it. It may be reassuring, however, to know something of what an experienced co-ordinator can eventually do.

So, back to the beginning. How will you take stock? If you have only been teaching a year and work alongside a lot of experienced staff, how do you gain the respect of these colleagues and get them to listen to you?

Policies, schemes of work and budgets

First of all become familiar with the school English and marking policies and its resources. Follow the policies and exploit the full range of resources available. Find out where everything is kept, ask people what they have in their classrooms (I was still finding things I did not know about after I had been in my present school for eighteen months, so do not feel bad if you have trouble finding things). If you know school policies and are implementing them, you are setting a fine example to the rest of the staff, which is a very good way to start. Find out if there is a budget. If so, how much is there to spend? Talk to the headteacher or a senior teacher about policies. Are you automatically told how much there is to spend? Can you spend it as you like or are there strings attached? Find out when your budget must be used up. The financial year may run to the end of March, but in reality, many schools are short of money by January, and if you have not spent money allocated to English by then, you may not be able to spend it at all!

Know your subject

Do read around your subject. I subscribe to a journal called *The Literacy Co-ordinator's File* which I have found invaluable. Professional journals like *Junior Focus* and *Junior Education* frequently contain articles dwelling on ideas for

English teaching and there will be more that you come across in your general reading. As English co-ordinator, you will routinely receive a wealth of literature through the post, informing you of state-of-the-art teaching materials as well as promoting 'new' ideas. All of these help to keep you informed and up-to-date. You will find that people will come to you for advice on teaching English. If you have kept your reading and knowledge of resources up-to-date, you will be a valuable storehouse of information for other staff.

As well as reading around your subject, attending courses is of the utmost importance to keep abreast of new initiatives. You may at first feel apprehensive about talking in staff meetings. A way of easing gently into discussion is to begin by just asking for two minutes of time to feedback a little information from a course you have attended. As your confidence increases you will gradually feel able to extend your contributions.

Gaining the respect of your colleagues

If you are asked a question you cannot answer, do take the trouble to find out what the answer is. If you return to a member of staff with information he or she has requested, your credibility in the eyes of that person is quickly raised. When people realise you will always follow up a request for information or ideas, you will be well on your way to establishing yourself as an effective co-ordinator. This is an especially potent ploy if you are young and/or have less experience of teaching than some of your colleagues, since you need to gain a degree of respect right from the start. You can of course also gain colleagues' respect by setting up, somewhere around the school, displays related to English, which can also help you 'sell' your ideas.

A model of excellence

What you do in your own classroom is important. If the children you teach are always enthusiastic about reading and writing and confident in speaking out, your colleagues will be curious as to why this is the case. You need to raise enthusiasm by being enthusiastic yourself. Your attitude will be infectious. It will 'rub-off' on both children and colleagues. If you always make learning objectives plain to children, write them on the board, refer to them during a lesson and return to them at the end, the children will know what they have to learn and are likely to progress in planned ways. I believe most children like to please. So by sharing your ambitions with them, they are very likely to give you what you want. Additionally, setting targets for each child, negotiated through discussion, will most definitely move on their learning. These targets should be specific. For example, they might include beginning each sentence in a different way, not using the word 'and' more than three times on a page, finding alternative words for 'said'. Once these targets have been securely achieved, then new ones should be set.

Noticing and listening

If colleagues notice that you are well-versed in your subject, realise you will follow up enquiries and that you have set up interesting English displays around the school, they are likely to visit your classroom to find out more about what you are doing. Then they will pay attention not just to your wall displays but to how you set about raising the quality of English work in your classroom. You may, for example, have novel ways of displaying books. You may list targets on your wall, or (as mentioned in the previous paragraph) pinpoint individual targets for children. Listen to what your colleagues and the children have to say about English generally. How do they feel about the subject? When you are on playground duty, keep an ear open for children's gossip. Are there certain classes always enthusing about poetry or who always seem to dislike anything to do with reading and writing? What is the children's attitude to group reading? In my own school, group reading is arranged so that children are split into groups of six as a maximum, each led by an adult, a teacher, classroom assistant or parent. Sessions last about half an hour, with approximately fifteen minutes spent reading around the group, and a further fifteen minutes spent discussing a text (for example, asking questions about it). If you try out this activity, you will find it helps to give you an insight into where there are strengths and weaknesses in the school in your subject. As mentioned above, if certain classes show pleasure in something they do in English, it is always worthwhile finding out what it is that helps to get them so excited and motivated.

Spreading good practice

Commenting on things you find are of a good standard is a 'sure-fire' way of getting others to try to reach the same standard. To illustrate: having commented in the staff room on one occasion about a display looking really good with a very attractive border, suddenly all the displays in the school had very attractive borders! Everyone likes praise and certainly there are times when we all feel that 'thank you' is not said often enough. Admitting to someone, 'I really like the way you did ... x ...' is guaranteed to ensure that the activity is repeated or, even better, built on and developed.

Planning

Every school has its own way of planning. However it is done, an English co-ordinator really needs to scrutinise everyone's English plans. One strategy for doing this is to have a file in the staff room where everyone puts his or her English plan for each week. Plans are thus easily accessible and present you with a clear picture of what is going on. Information gained in this way gives a very good foundation for your own developmental policy. Reading the plans over a period of time will help you not only to grasp what is happening but will help you discern any gaps in curriculum coverage. If there are gaps, you need to find out why. The reason may very likely reduce to a lack of resources. If this is so, and you have any of your budget left, you should be able to take steps to plug the gap.

Making English come alive

So you have been English co-ordinator for a few months, you have your feet under the table and you feel you have the respect and interest of your colleagues. You know what is going on around the school, you are familiar with the resources. What next? It is important to remember that English should be exciting. So, before progressing to monitoring, work-sampling, studying, analysing data and so on, maybe now is a good time to choose a range of strategies to raise levels of motivation and interest in the subject. I would not advocate you do everything I am about to suggest within any one year, but over a number of years you might well manage some or all of them.

Book week

What better way is there to foster a love of books and reading than through a 'book week'? Such a week is not difficult to organise, but it will take a little time. Perhaps you could ask your headteacher for half a day of non-contact time in order to set it up.

First of all locate a 'book fair'. In schools, this usually consists of opening and closing metal trolleys containing a wide range of both fiction and non-fiction books which can be sold with commission going to your own school. You will be inundated with literature about book fairs arriving as part of the mountain of advertising circulars you receive. If you are unsure which company to pick as a supplier, contact your local education authority and ask whom it recommends. Most companies will deliver a book fair on a Friday and collect it on the following Friday. As described above, a book fair is simply a large collection of books which children can purchase from wheeled trolleys. Any book fair will earn for you a percentage discount on sales, depending on the size of your takings. You can generally spend what you have made on more books for your school.

It is a good idea to arrange for each class to view the books for just about twenty minutes each on the day the books arrive. This taster will whet the children's appetites, and when they go home they will usually ask their parents for money to spend on books the following week. You will need to set up a timetable for a book week so that each class can spend about forty-five minutes browsing through what is supplied and purchasing any they would like. Book week, however, is more than just a book fair. You will need to integrate other activities during the week. For example, you might invite in poets or a drama group, an illustrator or an author. I always find arranging for about three events during a week works well, especially if they are varied and likely to appeal to children.

In addition, you could hold a fancy dress competition on themes such as 'My Favourite Book Character' or 'Science Fiction'. If children have a chance to show off their fancy dress in assembly, these could be judged as part of a light-hearted competition with books given as prizes. Alternatively, each year group might hold a competition, for example:

- design a bookmark;
- draw and describe a fantasy character;
- draw a poster to advertise the book week;
- write a short story, design a book cover etc.

Any of these competitions could have a book token as a prize. Two related ideas involve having a 'practical activities' afternoon, and inviting in specialists such as English advisers, lecturers or headteachers to share their knowledge and love of books with children. If planning a practical activity, the whole school could be split into small, differently aged groups. Activities might range from 'performance poetry' to writing recipes on a computer (perhaps using *Microsoft Publisher* software). If you are a member of a very brave team you could put on a performance of poetry and music for the children (staff in my present school did just this, and set a memorable example for the children). All these ideas are worth trying as ways of stimulating interest in literacy in a school. You will usually need to write letters to parents as well as asking for parent helpers – especially if you are going to open the book fair after school when children can drag their parents in to purchase more books! At one school where I taught, book week was organised during the same week as parent consultation evenings. As we held our book fair in the evenings, many parents came along to buy even more books!

Visiting a library

How many children in your school belong to the library? Your target should be every child! Many libraries are very happy to have classes visit and will arrange talks for the children to encourage them to join. It is well worth ringing up local librarians and asking what they are prepared to do free of charge. Some of our children who did not belong to a library, talked about their visit so persistently even the most reluctant parents felt compelled to enrol a son or daughter. It is well worth following library visits up in class, reminding children when a library is open, asking if anyone managed to borrow a particular book. You may well have provoked children not only to join a library but to relish the opportunity to read a wide range of books. If teachers do not take this initiative, many children would never actually *enter* a library let alone *enrol*!

Local and national competitions

There must be at least ten organised competitions coming through the post into a school each term. So the world is a co-ordinator's oyster really. Some competitions can be read about in the educational press and professional journals, but there will be many others advertised through leaflets posted to you as English co-ordinator. If you have been a co-ordinator for a while, you may feel confident enough to tell the children about a competition as part of a school assembly, or you may want to inform colleagues about it during staff meetings, asking them to pass on the news to their classes. You may even want to send a letter home. Whatever competitions you decide to enter, you will have found a new way to encourage the children's reading and writing by giving them a 'real' readership for their work. This is so important. Many competitions have prizes for schools as well as for individual pupils. The thrill of a child in winning a local or national competition is exciting not just for the individual but for the whole school.

A school website

Many schools now have their own website. A website is not just a way of advertising a school. It is much more than that (imagine the pride children feel at publishing some of their poetry on the school website). Children in one of my classes wrote some enjoyable and witty poems in the style of Roald Dahl, which we published on our website. The thrill expressed by those children (not to mention their parents) at their work being potentially accessed by anyone in the world was a joy to behold. The close involvement it aroused amongst the other children was equally valuable. The website (like competitions) gave child-poets a real audience for their work and stimulated others into believing that their work, too, could be published on it. It very quickly became a remarkably successful incentive for quality work. There is nothing quite like providing a readership outside school for children's work. The children will feel driven to producing work of an excellent standard as soon as they realise that – theoretically – anyone in the world can log onto a website and read what they write. In effect, they are becoming 'real' authors.

Producing a children's poetry book

Something that, as yet, I have not done, but would dearly love to do given enough time, is to make children into authors by including their work in a published book. Such an achievement would be a prime motivator and could be an enterprise open to a whole school. Although you (as co-ordinator) would be the editor, the venture could be yet another good way of engaging parents in the life of your school, in so far as you could ask qualified parents to help (one or two might do the illustrations, perhaps with help from children). You may be lucky enough to know parents who have contacts in the book publishing world. A school I taught in arranged for a book of children's poetry to be published by a publishing company. The children were so proud of their work, and the book sold very well to parents, grand-parents and so on. The fact that it is on sale in bookshops along with the work of 'real' authors is a terrific motivator for writing.

Children writing books for the school library or younger children

Again, this strategy gives to children a readership outside their own friends and relatives. Having looked with children at the features of non-fiction writing, I then set them the task over a six-week period of writing their own non-fiction book (with some time spent on it in school and some set as homework). I have worked through this idea with two classes and both times was impressed by the standard of work produced. Each book had to have a contents page, an index and a glossary. The children quickly became fascinated by the prospect of their work ending up in the school library, for anyone to borrow and read. The possibility really captured their imagination and fired them up. I was amazed at the lengths they went to in order to put their book together. Many put a picture of themselves as the author on the back of their book, adding a pen portrait of themselves. Some used a computer to sort out their glossary alphabetically, hence refining their IT skills at the same time. All had highlighted, or written in a different font, words meant to appear in the glossary, just as in adult non-fiction books. One child, who wrote a book on the human body, stuck velcro onto cut-out pieces of card shaped as various organs, so that these could be lifted in and out to reveal other organs underneath. Her book was heavily used when we studied a topic on the body later in the school year.

Class assemblies

While you are a new co-ordinator it is a good time for colleagues to become aware through a class assembly that you have innovative ways to improve children's love of writing, poetry, reading, speaking out and drama. It is probably a mistake for children to take a script into a class assembly, because there is always a temptation for them to read it and this often reduces the volume and expression of the children's voices. If you are in a school where classes do this you can help set a new trend by showing how well the children perform when they learn their words by heart. Colleagues will notice how your class speaks out. At the start of an assembly, I usually get my class to stand up one at a time and just shout the word 'hello!'. It might sound strange, but the ploy really works. Tell the children you want them to scream the word 'hello' at the top of their voices, just so that they can hear how loud they can be. If you give team points for the loudest voices, you will be amazed at the volume. Having done that, I get each child to shout 'My name is …!' We build up from there. You will find that even the shyest and quietest of children will be less afraid to speak out loudly and clearly. Having got them to use loud clear voices, you have jumped the highest hurdle.

As a new English co-ordinator, you may well think it a good idea to put on an assembly related to poetry, getting the children to act out part or the whole of a poem. Some poems could be recited in groups, or with children taking different parts. Some can be put to music composed by your class. The framework of the literacy hour gives many ideas for different types of poetry. Another idea I found worked well was to produce a simplified version of a Shakespeare play. One week during literacy hour, one of my classes acted out a quarter of a simplified version of *Macbeth* every day for four days. This was after I had told the children one quarter of the story each day. As well as listening to the story, they looked at overhead projector transparencies presenting a very simplified version of the play. On the fifth day, they put all four parts together. I was stunned at how much of Shakespeare's language they had taken on board. Their improvisations included vast amounts of the language, all used correctly. I hear from the secondary schools these children now attend that they have gone on to develop a love of Shakespeare and are not finding his writing difficult when they meet it. The parents of the children who came to watch the twenty-minute version of *Macbeth* during class assembly time, were amazed at the children's enthusiasm. Apparently, the children (including many with special needs) had been talking about it at home and were quoting lines to their parents.

Monitoring and evaluation

Once you feel you have established yourself as English co-ordinator, have the respect of your colleagues and have exploited one or two exciting ideas which help bring English to life, it is time to think about monitoring and evaluating!

What is monitoring?

It is

- finding out about what is happening in your school;
- checking to see if teachers are doing what they say they are doing;
- a process, which enables us to keep English 'on track' and which triggers new developments;
- about improving your school and not about accountability.

What do you look for when you are monitoring?

You look for

- standards across the school;
- coverage of the curriculum;
- consistency between classes;
- compliance with school policy;
- continuity and progression;
- evidence of differentiation;
- presentation and display;
- assessment, marking and feedback.

How do you monitor?

You monitor by

- work-sampling;
- observing;
- interviewing;
- looking at records;
- looking at SATS and teacher assessment;
- using questionnaires;
- looking at planning;
- listening;
- discussing;
- keeping a log/file.

Why do we monitor?

We monitor in order to gather information which we can evaluate. Without this process, there would be a lack of continuity and pace. I will take from the above list, in turn, each of the ways of monitoring I have not yet touched on.

Work-sampling

This is an excellent way of seeing what is really happening in classrooms. Is everyone really doing what they say they are doing? Is everyone putting school policies into practice? At my current school, we have an open-evening the night before parents' consultation evening. This not only allows parents to see work and displays around the school, but also subject co-ordinators can walk around a school and sample work. This process is something we find so effective that we carry it out three times a year.

Another way to work-sample is to collect in some work from every class according to a particular focus. You could, for example, ask for six books from each class representing work from two able, two average and two weak children, making your focus differentiation according to ability. By looking at books in this way, you will also be able to see if there is progression through a school. You might make your focus gender, and look at the work of three boys and three girls in each class. You can then decide whether boys and girls are reaching the same standards or whether there is a discrepancy. You need to be aware that some staff may find it threatening to have their work looked at in this way. It is up to you to set the monitoring process up in as tactful way as possible. You might well explain that as English co-ordinator it is very useful for you to know what is going on in the school. Also, work-sampling really does give you the opportunity to detect similarities and differences in achievement between classes which is very important if you have parallel classes.

Another way of sampling work is to share extended writing books in a staff meeting. I think it is good practice always to give feedback on a piece of extended writing with a positive comment plus a personal target. In my case, I mark the target with a sticky flag. These are, simply, very thin pieces of self-adhesive plastic two centimetres wide by four centimetres high. Their lower half is blank and sticks inside the child's book, the top half sticks out of the top as a flag. This ensures that every time the children write in these books, they can initially turn to their flag or flags in order to remind themselves of their personal targets. By setting them a personal writing target or two, they know what criteria are being used to mark their work. Because they want to please you, and because they are focused on what you want, they are likely to succeed in meeting their targets. Once a child has achieved his or her targets on a number of occasions (showing they have fully taken your teaching on board) it is time to set a new target or two, registering this with another flag. Telling the children they get a new flag when they have achieved a target and telling them the more they have the better is a way of maintaining motivation and involvement.

Sharing extended writing books in a staff meeting can be a very effective way of disseminating good practice. When teachers look at each other's way of marking, everyone can learn from each other. For example, it can be quite difficult setting targets challenging enough for the most able children. By studying each other's books, they can learn new and useful ideas. Since good practice is shared, standards should rise. The spin-off from this is that where practice is less good, colleagues concerned may become aware of this fact in a sympathetic, sharing setting. Good practice might, in such circumstances, rub off on those who need guidance – again, raising standards of marking and target setting.

Through discussions about work-sampling, a whole staff can agree to adopt any effective practices thought appropriate. Depending on how the meeting goes, you might compile a written report of where you feel you are with marking and target setting, and plan for further improvement by writing a list of 'next steps'.

Apart from looking at ability and gender across the year groups, as English co-ordinator, you might also take as a focus the special needs children in your school, or those with English as a second language. Alternatively, you could choose a random selection of children from a class register.

Observing lessons

As a new or experienced co-ordinator, observing lessons can be helpful in informing you about what is going on in school. If you are new, observations can be set up so that colleagues recognise that you are getting to know more about your subject. It is probably best to enter classrooms with intentions known and agreed between colleagues beforehand. Emphases could be placed on the structure and organisation of lessons, the way groups work, how special educational needs is incorporated in day-to-day teaching or gender issues. I always warn colleagues that I will be taking copious notes. My reasoning is that it can be useful for me to write down everything I see, as it is so easy to forget key observations afterwards. I can then write a general report on what my school has achieved so far. By reading the report carefully, and through discussion with colleagues at a staff meeting, an agreed list of 'next steps' can then be drawn up. Preserving a teamwork ethos is crucial. After reaching agreement, the report and list of next steps can be presented at an appropriate governing body committee, because it is important that governors know what is going on in the school. This procedure gives you a valuable opportunity to share with governors developments in English.

After compiling a list of 'next steps', it is useful to give a copy to everyone concerned and agree a date by which these should be in place. When the agreed date arrives, everyone can review their list and tick off what they have done, leaving blank what they have omitted. In the school where I teach, we found one integral step had been omitted by nearly everyone. In other words, through the process of monitoring we were able to rectify this deficit and decide what we needed to do to fill the gap.

Analysis of SATs and teacher assessments

Do get to know the Key Stage 1 and Key Stage 2 test and teacher assessment results. Talk with the assessment co-ordinator. It is worth checking on progression throughout a school. You might well also collaborate with an assessment co-ordinator to detect any patterns and trends over years. Look at the difference in results achieved by children according to when they were born during a year. Look at gender differences – are there issues here? If so, think of what you could do to redress any imbalance. If, for example, boys' reading is inferior to girls, you could try buying in more non-fiction books. Reportedly, boys prefer non-fiction to fiction. If summer-born children are not achieving as highly as the older children, more classroom assistant help can be targeted at the summer-born children. A school may choose the 'optional' end of Year 3, 4 and 5 SATs type tests. It is worth making a graph of the results so that you are aware of progression and where there may be strengths and weaknesses of achievement or provision.

Look too, at teacher assessments. Are they similar to the SATs results or are they a lot lower or higher? If lower, are expectations of children high enough? Do set targets help children to move on to the next level? Are your results above/below the county/national average? How do you compare with similar schools? Think about what you can put in place to raise standards.

Parental questionnaires

Parents are important to any school. It is very easy to get wrapped up in your own world and feel everything is going well, without really noticing the full picture. A good school self-evaluates in many ways. Finding out what parents think can be enlightening, and sometimes can bring about surprises. You might decide, for example, to canvass parents' opinions of the school reading programme. You could send out a letter with such questions as:

- What is the general impression of the success of the home-school reading programme?
- How does the guidance and reading record book help you know what to do?
- How suitable are the books your child brings home to read?
- How helpful are the comments made by the school?
- What improvements could be made in any of these areas?

Again, what matters is that when you receive the questionnaires back, you take time to analyse data and then, most crucially, set up a plan of action.

Children's questionnaires

Children's learning is what school is all about! So it is always a good idea to elicit children's opinions. You might design for them a similar questionnaire to that completed by parents, but written in 'childspeak'.

What is evaluation?

It is

- looking at what has been monitored in order to identify key strengths and weaknesses;
- about what is happening in your school, especially in relation to children's learning and achievement.

Why do we evaluate?

We evaluate in order to maintain the strengths of the school. We learn from our weaknesses so that we can then set up strategies to overcome them.

What happens to an evaluation report?

We intervene in the workings of our own schools on the basis of an evaluation report. We set up action plans with targets. These targets can then be incorporated into a school development plan.

How often should we evaluate?

It is important to evaluate regularly. Change is so rapid in English that it is hard to find the time to keep up to date with all the new initiatives. There are also unpredictable demands. Frequently there is no time to put new ideas and initiatives in place. Many schools have little money and there is little or no non-contact time for teachers to implement these ideas. Do not be too pessimistic however. As I write, there does seem to be more money coming in to schools and some of it does not have strings attached. There *is* light at the end of the tunnel!

What is helpful?

Make attainable goals for yourself and set them within a realistic time-scale. This gives you a real sense of achievement. Make sure you have the requisite resources, and that there is money available to get resources for any project you intend to undertake, whether it be organising non-contact time for monitoring, or planning a book week, or paying for a well known author or poet to speak to the children.

Why is it enjoyable to be an English co-ordinator?

The possible reasons for anyone enjoying the co-ordination of English are endless. The sheer excitement of bringing about a life-long love of reading, writing or drama is enough in itself. You can manage this through the enthusiasm you bring to your role. There are so many exciting things you can do in a school to lift achievements in English. The thrill of children having their work published in a book, displayed on the school website, entering competitions, dressing up as a book character to parade in front of a school are rewarding experiences which make teaching English fun and memorable.

As well as organising enjoyable opportunities for children to learn co-ordinating English offers substantial opportunities for professional development. It is really up to you how far you develop the role. I hope when you have read this chapter, and tried out a few of its ideas, you will, like me, discover just how much you can do, not only to develop yourself professionally, but to have a real impact on the rest of the school. If you can give to the children (not just in your class) a lifelong love of learning, then you have achieved your aim. What could be more satisfying to any teacher?

6. Excellence in the Teaching of English to Bilingual Children

Tim Parke

Introduction

The aim of this chapter is to look at factors likely to assist teachers in helping their bilingual pupils towards excellent understanding and use of English. The chapter has six main sections. It starts by looking at the following questions: What does bilingualism mean? Who is bilingual and how many bilingual pupils are there in schools? It then examines influences on the language development of bilingual children such as the importance of language models, children's position in their families and the 'language policies' of their homes. Next, two case studies where young bilingual children are seen operating in educational settings are described: in the first study, we find them telling stories from pictures; in the second, producing narratives. Finally, implications for reaching excellence in teaching these children the understanding and production of English are spelled out.

Bilingualism: definitions

What is bilingualism? One problem is that there are too many answers to this question. It is possible to take a strictly linguistic view and repeat the American linguist Bloomfield's judgement in 1933 that people are bilingual who have 'native-like control' of the two languages in question (Bloomfield did not consider more than two languages). What this definition amounts to is that a bilingual person is like two monolinguals in one brain/body. Everything he or she can say in language A, he or she can say in language B. In fact, even the most competent bilinguals commonly reveal two things in their language behaviour: that they have strengths and weaknesses in the way they use each of their languages, that they automatically use one language rather than the other in certain circumstances. A good example of this common feature of bilingual performance arises when referring to so-called 'internal speech', which we use when doing things like calculating, following precise routines (setting up a mobile phone), and praying. Bilinguals frequently revert (that is, 'internally') to their first-learned language in such situations.

Bloomfield's definition also implies that bilingualism is solely a question of language. To a linguist who is principally interested in the mental processes associated with language, this implication might be correct. A sociolinguist interested in bilingualism would look more closely at issues such as language and power; *who* uses which language with *whom*; what functions a language might have for its speakers, and other factors going beyond the psychological features of individuals. Similarly, bilingualism presents teachers and educationalists with issues where a number of such human factors (that is, with a social dimension) must be taken into account. Any definition must refer to matters wider than the purely linguistic.

To be more precise: as well as being a 'code', a set of symbols that we can order and re-order to convey meaning, language has a role as an emblem of social and personal identity. We can grasp this by considering how any one of us might answer the telephone. Within less than a second, we process a mass of information – whether we know the caller or not, his or her gender, age, accent. Consequent upon this information, we assess the caller's class, education, occupation and purpose in calling. Language – speech, in this example – is a stream of information that does not just *say* something for purposes of communication; it also says something *about* the speaker. This is important when considering bilingualism because we have to understand that the 'knowledge *how*' of speakers (their ability to produce language to a given level) is one thing, while their 'knowledge *of*' a language they are using (its resonances, attributes, roles, history, community) is another. To simplify radically: children whose productive capacity in a language is no more than an ability to utter a small number of ritual greetings or farewells may still, when asked, classify themselves as a speaker of the language merely by virtue of allegiance to the community the language represents.

I propose, then, an inclusive definition of bilingualism, allowing for both dimensions outlined above, incorporating two levels of meaning. The level of ability to produce (speak, communicate and so on), and the level of identi-fication with a community are, somehow, combined. Awareness of both is needed by teachers who wish to assure that these children achieve their full potential in English.

Who are they?

The number of bilingual children in British schools is still a matter of con-jecture, as local education authorities are not obliged to conduct surveys of languages spoken by children in their schools (though some do). In addition to this, the fact of transient populations, such as refugees and asylum seekers, some of whom may be incipient bilinguals but whose numbers are difficult to estimate, has to be remembered. It is noteworthy that the index of the most extensive recent survey of ethnicity in the United Kingdom (Parekh, 2000), does not contain a reference to 'language(s)'.

We do, however, have reliable figures for some areas of Britain, and, pretty inevitably, London is one of them. Table 6.1 below shows the 'top forty' languages spoken in the capital (from Baker and Eversley, 2000), ranging from 600,000 English speakers to 450 speakers of Sinhala, the official language of Sri Lanka. There is a marked split between the table's two halves, corresponding more or less to a division between the older, well-established languages and more recent arrivals. We know from Stubbs (1985) that languages such as Turkish, Greek and Italian have been taught within and by their respective communities for several decades, while the numbers for Russian, Pashto, Tigrunya and Albanian reflect more recent population movements. A notable exception to this division (between the growth of well-established and least-established languages) is the figure for Bengali/Sylheti speakers. Although one would have expected such a language to have become well established and have been widely spoken over many years in Britain, speakers only began to appear in large numbers during the last twenty years of the twentieth century. Such figures lead us into a number of important issues. First, there is the question of identifying child-speakers of languages other than English. The first knowledge a school may have of the presence of such children is when they turn up on day one (there may be no adult on a staff who can identify the language, let alone communicate in it). Then there is the question of 'language claiming'. There may well be cases of over- or under-reporting language use, as when a parent claims that *only* a certain language is spoken in his or her home, or, conversely, that a certain language

Table 6.1: The top forty mother tongues in London

	Language	approx. numbers		Language	approx. numbers
1	English	608,500	21	Igbo	1,900
2	Bengali and Sylheti	40,400	22	French-based Creoles	1,800
3	Panjabi	29,800	23	Tagalog (Filipino)	1,600
4	Gujarati	28,600	24	Kurdish	1,500
5	Hindi/Urdu	26,000	25	Polish	1,400
6	Turkish	15,600	26	Swahili	1,000
7	Arabic	11,000	27	Lingala	1,000
8	English-based Creoles	10,700	28	Albanian	900
9	Yoruba	10,400	29	Luganda	800
10	Somali	8,300	30	Ga	800
11	Cantonese	6,900	31	Tigrinya	800
12	Greek	6,300	32	German	800
13	Akan (Ashanti)	6,000	33	Japanese	800
14	Portuguese	6,000	34	Serbian/Croatian	700
15	French	5,600	35	Russian	700
16	Spanish	5,500	36	Hebrew	650
17	Tamil	3,700	37	Korean	550
18	Farsi (Persian)	3,300	38	Pashto	450
19	Italian	2,500	39	Amharic	450
20	Vietnamese	2,400	40	Sinhala	450

Source: (Baker and Everly, 2000)

is not spoken there at all. The explanation for this apparent subterfuge may be that if speakers expect support to be forthcoming as a result of the enquiry, they will disclose the language(s) for which support is needed. If, however, the information obtained is likely to provoke unwelcome attention (for example in how that home might be perceived within the school system), they may play down the facts of differential language use.

The third issue is, precisely, that of arranging appropriate support. Even within the relatively circumscribed area of London, the chances of matching children who speak a particular language to an adult who speaks it, still less a teacher, are in many cases small. Inevitably, the most serious causes for concern are those where small numbers of children live in relatively isolated situations. For example, where there are few adult speakers of their language either in the school or the community, few opportunities are likely to exist for the children to develop their principal tongue. The issue of teacher supply is directly related to this. Providers of teacher education have often thought it not worthwhile to run courses where the 'target population' is either small, or transient, or both (Craft and Atkins, 1985). Rules on the recognition of international degrees and admission to the teaching profession in the United Kingdom are strict. One effect of this limited provision within teacher education and restrictions on the supply of some bilingual teachers has been the formation of a small 'sub-class' of sometimes very skilled and experienced individuals (reckoned at about 3,000 across Britain) working alongside teachers as bilingual classroom assistants (Hugh South, personal communication, May 2001).

Language development in the bilingual home

I turn, now, to 'the beginning of the story': the language development of young bilingual children before they attend school. What follows necessarily involves generalising from imaginary cases but it is thought valid to extrapolate from the cases described, provided these have sufficient verisimilitude to be accepted as representative of real circumstances, and provided one generalises cautiously, making tentative propositions rather than hard and fast claims.

I will take the case of a young child born into a family where there are two parents and a number of other adults (grandparents perhaps, and possibly older children). I will make the assumption, simply for this illustration, that the adults share at least one home language, that some of them have a better knowledge of English than others have, and that the children are attending an 'English-medium' school. This could be a school where there is either a minority or a majority of speakers of language other than English, but where the curriculum, as is legally required, is delivered in English. My central question is this: What might the language socialisation of such an individual look like?

One obvious feature of the child's general language environment will be its multi-lingual nature. Adults are likely to speak to each other in their home language (to simplify, I will assume they have only one), and grandparents may only speak this language. It will be natural for the adults, at least at the beginning of a child's life, to communicate with her or him in this language – not through any deliberate decision, but because natural language-use comprises, as we have seen, the twin aspects of communication and identity. To bring up children is to introduce them into a community, and the prime way of doing this is to pass on one's language. A language functioning domestically will probably not be the only one used. English will pervade the home both in the form of mass media (though newspapers, films, letters and so on may be in the home language) and in the form of the English brought back by older siblings. The work of Gregory (1996) showed something of the role siblings have in transmitting to young children the language and literacy practices of a 'host' community.

Further, given the presence of two languages in a home – admittedly, contributing unequally to discussions and probably at differing levels of competence – it is likely that language-mixing will occur. This latter concept pins down the way in which items from two languages combine either within the same piece of discourse (for example, within a conversation, or within single utterances forming the conversation). The reasons for mixing (sometimes called 'code-switching') are various, but it is useful to realise that, in itself, such mixing is neither a consequence of ignorance nor an indicator of confusion. Where a child knows a term only in one language, it is logical that he or she should use it even when contributing to a discussion beginning in the other language. The alternative is for the child to abandon any impulse to communicate. Another motivation in switching may be to include a newcomer in a conversation; or, again, to talk about a topic, such as school-work, familiar to participants in one language and not the other. In the early years of primary school, language-mixing is sometimes taken by teachers as evidence that a child is confused or unable to distinguish between the two languages used. There is still extant evidence that health visitors and speech therapists continue to advise parents to bring up a child in one language, not two, in order to avoid such confusion (Zentella, 1997).

This brings us to a discussion of language policy in the home. In some families, no such thing as a thought-out policy exists when a child is born – especially a first child. It may only be when parents notice influences on their child's language that they begin to reflect on desirable long-term outcomes. In other families, it may be taken for granted that certain language practices will be instituted. For example, attendance at Koranic/Qu'ranic school entails a child learning Arabic from a particular type of model. In whatever way it comes about, there will always be something we can loosely refer to as a 'policy' being followed, and this policy will be fashioned by a mixture of conscious decisions and pragmatic considerations.

Adherence to a religion (already mentioned) is clearly a conscious decision. So is the desire for literacy in a home language (if it is one with a written form). Other factors may be a family's long-term aim to return to a home country. They may also include shorter-term aims of adults wanting children to be able to communicate with relatives during holidays to a home country; and a more general desire simply to pass on the home country's language, culture and heritage. A more circumstantial matter is the presence in the home of adults who may only be able to speak a home language, and who can therefore only communicate with a younger generation in this way. If we look at the question from an English-teaching perspective, we need to see how these factors interact in the lives of children moving regularly between home and school environments.

The first point is that there is no template for producing successful learners, whatever their language background. Any child coming to school for the first time is both a product of a number of social influences and a potential active individual learner whose capacities cannot be predicted by any genetic calculation. In the same way, there is no template for a successful bilingual. While on the one hand there is good evidence that the practice of 'one person, one language' can lead to balanced bilingualism in children (Zentella, 1997) there is also evidence that 'balanced' bilinguals can emerge from situations where languages are mixed at home (Goodz, 1994). Teachers are simply not in a position to have much say about any of this. *How* they teach can be informed significantly by their understanding of the processes their pupils have experienced within domestic settings.

A final factor to be considered in this first analysis is how the pupils' communities view their roles. Returning to the dual definition of language as both a 'code' and an 'emblem of personal and social identity', we must be aware that what parents and carers bestow on a school are children holding their own successfully (at least to a degree) within community norms, which include linguistic norms. A low level of achievement in spoken English, relative to monolingual peers, is only one – usually a school's – way of seeing a child. What parents may see is a fully socialised individual, with abilities in one or more languages, very far from disadvantaged when it comes to learning another. In fact, there is sound evidence (Parke and Drury, 2001) that at least some communities see English teaching as the preserve of a school system, and not something to which attention should be devoted before a child enters it. The 'disadvantage' the school perceives may lie in the fact that young, potentially bilingual children will not have had several years of mainstream school-type literacy activities. They will not have been read to in English, told stories such as English fairy-stories, handled books written in English with associated script conventions, that is, reading from left-to-right and top-to-bottom (SCAA, 1996: 3). Obviously, this lack of culture-specific experiences is not found solely with bilingual children, which is as true of any child whose home background does not mesh neatly with that of the school. I return to this point in my final section.

Language from home to school

This section examines in general terms some of the distinctive differences between the language of a home and that of a school found in the situations of bilingual children. It is a truism to say that most children's home language tends to express the here-and-now (Foster-Cohen, 1990). From the earliest age, children's language development is grounded in what is physically present, developing from eye-contact and gesture, and moving on to the naming of recurring physical objects in an immediate environment. It is when they are around the age of eighteen months that, classically, adults begin to play 'peek-a-boo' games with toddlers, giving children faith in the existence of objects temporarily invisible. This process is typically one-to-one (dyadic): a child is often addressed by a single adult or older sibling. It is easy for children to focus on the activity, which is physical, and on their partners in the activity. Language grows naturally out of these activities. It seems, at first, that we do not so much teach language to children as treat them as viable communicators, and that the language develops 'on the back of' the communication.

As it does so, it begins to develop through fairly well-documented phases up to the age of five or so, by which stage most children have acquired basic systems requiring relatively minor elaboration to cope with adult demands. This fairly neat account may sound extremely straightforward. However, it is worth recalling that, while the scene is changing rapidly, the vast majority of work carried out on child language acquisition has been done on children acquiring English (for example, Brown, 1973; Gleason and Berko, 1989). Moreover, there has been a tendency to transfer findings (for example, identifying so-called 'stages') not simply from English to other languages, but from the development of monolingual capabilities to the development of bilingual capabilities. Brief reflection shows that a child acquiring two languages simultaneously experiences very different processes and circumstances from those experienced by a monolingual child. Indeed, one feature bedevilling the assessment of young bilinguals has been the tendency to import monolingual norms into a bilingual situation.

Language in the home, then, is characterised by its being embedded in a presently occurring physical reality. It is also characterised as being under the control of its speakers, and by its typical discourse-patterns. However, although the home language derives from a here-and-now activity, there may be no obligation on a child to continue that activity beyond his or her natural attention span. Similarly, children are able to *choose* whether to contribute to a conversation or not. They will be most used to a one-to-one pattern of discourse – probably untypical of much school discourse. Finally, there is the issue of literacy. Huge variations are apparent in the literacy experiences of young children within their homes, ranging from the experiences of those who are fluent readers to those who have little skill in handling books, let alone decoding them. Some have concepts of literacy varying sharply from that of a mainstream school (Hirst, 1998).

Significant changes occur when a child enters school at around the age of five. Probably the greatest of these concern conceptual development. It is easy to imagine a child who, on entering school, has a wide range of stored experiences and some means of talking about them. Very typically at this age, children have difficulty with 'pronominal' reference. That is, they may find it hard to choose pronouns in such a way as to make meaning sufficiently explicit and unambiguous. Many teachers become familiar with this when children begin to produce written texts using 'he' or 'she' to refer to more than one individual (Perera, 1984). More noteworthy than this aspect of conceptual and linguistic behaviour is the gradual crystallising in children's minds of categories within which they can locate past and present events. For example, a child may know about seemingly unconnected experiences such as a holiday, a postcard from overseas, a parent having a day off work, a sibling going to work for the first time, and so on. What happens as a result of schooling is that children develop sets of abstractions linked to this knowledge, such as 'work' and 'leisure', enabling them to connect the separate events and thus organise and store them together. This allows memory to operate successfully through connections being established between events, people and objects. It represents the beginnings of a conceptual framework within which the child can organise new experiences.

This happens naturally through the use of special language forms, that is, the 'umbrella' terms or abstractions that name concepts. The issue for young bilinguals is that, whether or not they have been developing two languages in the home, or a single, predominant one, they may not have registered certain dimensions of experience in ways and in a language which the school can access. Neither their vocabularies nor their experiences may match those of their monolingual peers. Furthermore, languages differ in the ways they categorise the world. Admittedly, the issue is contentious: the now notorious story involving Inuits enjoying multiple words for different types of snow has long been discredited (Pinker, 1994). Nevertheless, there is a substantial point to make. If concepts differ from one language to another, so must vocabularies. A good illustration to reveal the implied correspondence between conceptual and linguistic/cultural development is the way the colour spectrum is seen to differ even between the historically and geographically close communities of France and the United Kingdom. The way colours are perceived, and therefore classed as 'blue' or 'green', is not, simply, a matter of agreement. It must engage actual divergences in the way communities conceptualise (and therefore interpret and speak about) their culturally-related experiences of colour.

Another change occurring as part of conceptual development is in discourse patterns. As well as becoming more abstract, enabling children to refer not only to what is present but to the past and possible futures, language in school becomes more public and in some ways more controlled than it is prior to their entering school. Talk must at least sometimes be public, and must often be about topics teachers have selected. Children have to get used to addressing given subjects in front of their class-mates. So, spoken language comes increasingly under public scrutiny. As it happens, children are very sensitive to how one person's speech differs from another. Initially, they will notice differences in accent, then differences of vocabulary and syntax. Such growing awareness is part of their realisation that, in school, language is an object in its own right, open to comment and criticism. For young bilinguals, an initial low attainment in English, however temporary, is likely to be for them a (possibly stigmatising) mark of difference.

We come finally to the question of literacy. For some children, school literacy (setting aside initiatives such as the literacy hour) is just a matter of 'more of the same'. Stories, characters, purpose, language, script, the way a book is jointly read, commented on and elaborated is part-and-parcel of their daily lives. Not least, the culturally specific way in which books are conceived, remain consistent between home and school. For many young bilinguals, as Gregory (1996) has shown, literacy is a quite different 'kettle of fish'. Far from it being a matter for them of identifying or empathising with characters, of gaining some sort of comprehension and being entertained or soothed, reading a book may actually be a matter of deep cultural and/or religious significance. It may be subject to specific settings and rituals, with relatively little expectation that the construction of personal meanings (that is, specific to the individuals concerned) plays much part in an overall reading activity.

The language of young bilinguals: two examples

I turn now to a pedagogical focus on 'excellence'. Having set out a background against which language may develop in bilingual homes, and noted important differences between home and school, I give some contrasting examples of the language produced by children in school. My aim is to show how teachers can listen to and analyse what is actually going on, before devising strategies to improve performance.

Picture stories

Picture stories are a tried-and-tested means by which teachers assess the language level of young children (Hedberg and Westby, 1993; Heras, 1994; Hoff-Ginsberg, 1997). These stories have the apparent advantage that they already exist 'out there': they do not have to be constructed from scratch. For a teacher, the advantage of turning to a picture story task is that it gives a context in which language will occur naturally. It allows the teacher to make contextualised judgements about children: first, about their talents for narration and, second, about other sub-systems such as pronunciation or vocabulary. In turn, children can assume that a listener engaged by the narrative has a basic model of what a story is, so his or her task is simply to make explicit a particular example. The burden of invention is apparently light.

Unfortunately, in the event, a child may make no such assumption. Since the book being used is placed in front of both child and teacher, the aim of the activity may actually be obscure to the child (Meek, 1988). Conversely, the aim may seem all too obvious. Since so much is carefully arranged, the child may sense all too clearly that the focus of the task is to test language capability. Adults usually assume that a story is derived effortlessly from the pages of a picture-book and that the circumstances in which a story is told matter little. We choose to forget the culturally rooted element of narrative, whether revealed in words or via some other medium (Heath, 1983).

In the work reported on here (see Parke, 2001), eight children, between the ages of seven years and eleven months and eight years and five months, were given the task of telling the story *Donald and the singing fish* taken from the picture-book of that name (Lubach, 1992). Four were monolingual English-speakers; one had Urdu as a first language; one had Farsi, and two had Gujerati. All had attended the same primary school in north-west London from the age of five. Research aimed to investigate two issues. The first was how the bilingual children coped with particular difficulties such as not knowing certain words that are key to re-telling the story, that is, their 'lexical strategies'. The second (not discussed here) was whether the teacher interacted differently with the different groups.

The text of course is overtly bizarre, but it was chosen to be bizarre for all participants. It shows, in pictures, the main character Donald trying to practise his bagpipes out at sea in a boat. The music attracts a fish that sings to his accompaniment. Donald and the fish return to land together and become a performing duo. Donald takes the fish home and buys a bowl for it to live in. The news gets round the town and, eventually, an impresario signs up the fish up to perform on stage. On its first night, the fish gets stage-fright. The audience is about to walk out when Donald saves the day by playing his bagpipes to accompany the fish.

The children used in the research were all seen separately by a teacher they knew well, and asked to 'tell the story'. All were happy to do so, though one child asked if he was 'doing it the same as all the others'. Researchers expected there to be differences in how the two groups of children responded to the task's challenges – particularly to their not having certain words in their vocabulary. But they had no clear expectations of how they would solve these problems. The following excerpts illustrate their strategies.

The first strategy, used by both sets of children, was to describe or define unknown items:

> Child 1:   'He went to the pet shop to get a … um … <u>thing with water</u> for him.' (Target item: bowl)

> Child 1:   'Then everyone put up posters outside the cinema to watch … um … <u>the show of the fish</u>.' (Target item: performance)

> Child 7:   'He took them to … a … <u>big house</u> where everyone can see him sing …' (Target item: theatre)

Table 6.2: Informants

Informant	Age (years; months)	First Language	Gender
1	8; 5	Urdu	f
2	8; 3	Gujerati	f
3	8; 6	Gujerati	m
4	8; 2	Farsi	m
5	8; 5	English	m
6	8; 1	English	m
7	8; 3	English	f
8	7; 11	English	f

The second strategy, which was more typically used by the bilingual children, was to substitute a known item for one that can be presumed unknown. Thus in the first example, the child does not know the word 'bagpipes':

Teacher: 'Do you want to turn the page and see what he [Donald] did with it [bagpipes]?'

Child 2:   '<u>Music</u>.'

Another child had a partial realisation of the target term:

Child 1:   'He took out his <u>Scottish pipes</u>. He played his <u>Scottish pipes</u>, and then ...'

A third, lesser-used strategy, was to 'grammaticalise' (e.g. change a known noun into a verb).

Child 1:   'He got out a wheelbarrow and <u>wheelbarrowed</u> it home.'

A fourth technique was to use a pronoun (even where antecedent for the pronoun has not been given).

> Child 1:   'He went to the pet shop to get a … um … thing with water for him then Donald went to the fish and he brought <u>one</u> … and <u>it</u> was brand new but …'

Informant 4 is, by far, the prime user of this latter strategy. Three instances occur within his first two turns where he is setting up the narrative. Not knowing four key lexical items is not going to stop him:

> Child 4:   'There was a boy was in the home, he was going to the fishing and then he put <u>this</u> [anchor] on the water and then he got <u>this</u> [the suitcase], and then he opened <u>this</u> [suitcase] and got <u>this</u> [bagpipes] … He … he … throw <u>this</u> [anchor] and then there was a singing.'

By comparison, monolingual children, while knowing more of a core vocabulary needed to make the story, typically had different strategies when it came to words they did not know. They tended to use the teacher more directly as source of knowledge, sometimes simply asking her directly:

> Child 5:   'What're they called?'

> Child 6:   'What are they called?'
>   'Is that a quaver?'
>   'Is he going to choke?'
>   'What's he doing?'

At other times, showing a more subtle awareness of teacher/pupil roles, they fall silent – and the teacher obligingly fills the gap:

> Child 8:   'One day there was a little boy, and he went fishing and he pulled the anchor up, and he opened his suitcase. And he got his …'

> Teacher: 'Bagpipes.'

Thus, in essence:

- bilingual children use a slightly wider range of strategies than mono-linguals – five separate types, as against three;
- all children use periphrasis, and to the same degree;
- only monolingual children ask the teacher a direct question; mono-linguals prompt their teachers more;
- only one child (bilingual) grammaticalises, and only one (bilingual) uses pronouns to render unknown items.

Table 6.3 shows differences in strategies found across the two groups. To sum up: bilingual groups are showing more language-based strategies than the monolingual, but monolinguals have more pragmatic strategies: they have more confidence in asking or prompting the teacher.

Table 6.3: Lexical strategies: by individual and by group

	1	2	3	4	EAL[a] group totals	FLE[b] group totals	5	6	7	8
Prompt teacher	1	0	1	0	2	6	0	2	2	2
Ask teacher	0	0	0	0	0	3	0	3	0	0
Periphrasis	4	0	1	0	5	5	3	0	2	0
Substitute	2	1	1	0	4	0	0	0	0	0
Grammaticalise	1	0	0	0	1	0	0	0	0	0
Pronoun	1	0	0	5	6	0	0	0	0	0
Individual totals	9	1	3	5	18	14	3	5	4	2

[a]EAL: English as an additional language
[b]FLE: first language English

Non-literal language

My second example involves a narrative of a different sort. The narrator here is a 10-year-old Bangladeshi girl in a north London primary school. Her first language is Sylheti (the non-written language of a northern rural province of Bangladesh). Her text is an 'oralised' version of a story (recorded on to tape) which she had written under the title "A Magic Journey Underground". In summary, the writer/teller wakes up 'one fine morning' and wants to go straight outside. Her mother sends her to tidy her room. Alone and bored, she notices a crack in the wall and digs away at it, uncovering a secret passage, stairs, an underground room, and, finally a wonderful banquet. Having eaten her fill, the story is turned into a dream, and she wakes up.

The interest here lies in the 10-year-old's figurative language. We make a distinction between language used simply for referring to things, and the non-literal use of language where we can choose the words we use and create special effects by exercising this choice. Children's initial use of language, as many writers (for example Halliday, 1975) have noted, is largely for labelling and so identifying people and things. Alongside the development of such systems as syntax and phonology however is pragmatic ability: the skills of understanding and using words with suitable sensitivity to context and to other speakers. Words cease to be simple labels and gain shared associations. Thus, to someone who shares a child's most intimate world, the word 'book', which begins as a label for a known object, can acquire all kinds of connotations. It becomes a request for a book, general or specific, to be read. It may indicate that a child is ready to go to bed. It can be a sign that a child has seen an animal he or she originally came to recognise from a book. It can mean the place where the book should be, but is not. These possibilities represent first strands of the development of a figurative language where words mean more than they say. They are key aspects of an appreciation of the language of literature.

Table 6.4 gives the main examples of non-literal language found in this text as put together by the child studied. We can look at them in two ways. The first is to look closely at their form. The other is to see them as devices deliberately chosen by this child to insert in a personal, imaginative narrative. In the table, columns 3 to 6 give noteworthy examples of separate aspects of language. Phrases, vocabulary, word-order are self-evident. By 'discourse move', is meant a strategy for structuring (here, terminating) the story.

Table 6.4: Examples of non-literal language

	Example	Phrase	Categories vocabulary	word-order	Discourse move
1	the sun's rays burning on my window	X			
2	I quickly got up			X	
3	Meekly		X		
4	With slime dripping in certain places	X			
5	Chamber		X		
6	From place to place	X			
7	I suddenly grew tired			X	
8	a table groaning with the weight of food	X			
9	so I tucked myself in	X			
10	this is going to be a nice lunch		X		
11	Sleepy, sleepy ...				X
12	Suddenly I woke up				X

Looking at language forms, there is plainly something non-standard about some of these examples. Is the target form for (1) 'burning *through* my window'? 'On' is not quite right. In (4), the expression ends weakly, as though the right words had not been found, and (9) looks like a combination of two expressions: 'to tuck in' (to a meal), and 'to be tucked up' (in bed). However let us turn to what works. In the first place, this is a narrative with a plain, strong structure. It has an everyday beginning, a fantasy middle section, and a down-to-earth ending. The writer/teller skilfully uses devices to get her from one episode to another – falling asleep, and waking up: the words 'sleepy, sleepy ...' repeated several times on the tape show that she can use this familiar discourse device to conclude her text. In other words, we see a learner at a fascinating, transitional stage of producing English. At the level of text, she has no problems, and is ready to develop fresher and more original ways of getting from one episode to another. At the level of grammar (which is not our concern here) there were no difficulties: for example, her use of tenses was correct and well adapted to her purposes. It is her vocabulary that is interesting, and shows three things. Most significantly, she has absorbed from her reading a number of items of figurative language. Second, she can use them in a suitable text-type. Third, she needs to consolidate and develop expressions she has acquired so as to deploy a more accurate idiomatic lexicon.

Implications for teaching

I have spent time in discussing elements of the language background of bilingual learners, given that understanding these must underpin how we assess their language performance in school. In my examples of school-based discourse, I have tried to show the processes that such pupils may have used in coming to terms with the demands of English in typical school situations. It is now time to tease out implications.

There are many variables at work in homes where two languages are being acquired, and it is impossible to make hard-and-fast predictions about what the competence in English of a young bilingual entering primary school will be like. Many teachers will be able to think of children apparently being brought up in situations which make their language development relatively predictable. Such children may, for example, be centres of attention in the home, may be spoken to in structured conversations, have learned turn-taking skills, have been read to and be able to read simple texts on entering school. As well as being commonplace features of these children's lives, such circumstances happen to be reliable predictors of general educational success. So a first important implication of closely studying the home lives of pupils is that, while we accept that connected factors make it likely that language performance will be a success, we need to search also for alternative models. We must do this so as not to promote a single route to linguistic excellence, because of the real danger that the monolingual model described above, refined and polished within the educational system for many years, will become a normative model, inevitably disadvantaging bilingual learners.

Moreover, let us insist, it is possible for bilingual children to achieve comparable levels of success. Teachers should consider in detail the special factors (some discussed in this chapter), specific to bilingual language development, and see how they work for the learners they are dealing with. Teachers need to recognise and understand children who have highly complex sets of linguistic interactions in their home, dealing with a number of languages, language-partners, literacies and even experiences of parallel schooling in a community school. Such circumstances seem complex and intricately interwoven with a number of intervening variables.

However, complexity and a range of variables affecting performance do not of themselves preclude secure learning outcomes, though they make it more difficult for teachers to assess how each variable affects individual learners. After all, it is not just the variables that matter. Equally important is what families make of them. How do *they* see their own multilingualism in the context of a predominantly monolingual society and educational system? How do *they* construct school literacy, which to them may seem to be predicated on the selfish enjoyment and individual interpretation of texts? In short, what is *their* language policy? As yet, there is little to go on in trying to answer these questions.

An extension of an approach centred on the practicality of teachers following more than one route to excellent practice concerns the role that a home language plays for bilingual children. A number of different strands to this topic have been discerned. One is the cultural significance that language has for communities. Almost regardless of actual levels of proficiency, community members may want to be seen as 'speakers of x', and this must be understood by others. It does not have to follow that such members want to have a curriculum delivered in their own language; self-identification is more to do with culture and heritage than language itself. So while acknowledging the significance of individual languages at the curricular level, we should be cautious about insisting it be applied to curriculum delivery.

A second strand is the actual function a home language has for children in school. Language functions are notoriously diverse. Policy in Britain makes support for a child's first language generally available (for example from bilingual classroom assistants, up to Year 1). Yet such support is temporary and transitional, with an emphasis placed on children working wholly in English as soon as possible. Recent work has shown that while some children cope well with this emphasis and function almost exclusively in English from Year 2 onwards, for others the home language is the main source of cognitive and linguistic input during a much longer period (Parke and Drury, 2001). Going beyond this position, successful examples of children working in their home language in a school classroom can be cited, for example at Regents Park Primary School, Birmingham (Levis, 2001). For such children, 'working in groups' normally means working in language groups; while discussions, story-telling and role-play happen whenever possible in the children's home languages. The co-existence of several languages in a classroom is seen as a norm.

We do not fully grasp the mechanisms that allow children in complex bilingual situations to cope well with school demands; but we know that some children do cope. So the second implication to be derived from the discussion is that careful and rigorous assessment of young bilinguals is needed as they enter school. Information from any early years provision is crucial and, with ever greater stress being placed by politicians (and others) on educating a highly qualified workforce, there is reason to expect early years practitioners to become increasingly sophisticated in noticing and noting the language development of children in their care. Teachers themselves need to collect a range of language samples from different settings. Some standard, well-attested assessments are highly structured (for example: certain vocabulary tests, such as the British Picture Vocabulary Test, in which the child is shown a picture of a 'familiar' object and has to name it).

However, these tests are notoriously culturally biased and great care has to be taken not to give too much weight to a child's inability to recognise or name what is, perhaps, an everyday kitchen object familiar to most monolinguals. Another type of assessment, also tightly structured, is grammatical assessment, where we are looking at a child's knowledge of English word-order and morphology. It is likely that in tests such as these, standardised on monolingual populations, bilingual children will achieve relatively low scores. The task of acquiring two languages nearly always takes longer than acquiring one, and thus monolingual norms, whether applied to children's additional language/English or to their first/'home' language, can be misleading. Such assessments do at least indicate levels of attainment at the time they were made but do not give a reliable measure of ability or potential.

Alongside these standardised tests are those that teachers might devise for themselves. These can be extremely informal, and are none the less valuable for that. While it is important to know with some precision just what words and structures a child can use competently, it matters just as much to know how children use language in natural situations. The following is a list of suggestions for this sort of informal monitoring:

- listening in to conversations between peers and building up, over a period of time, a knowledge of vocabulary, verb formations, pronunciation, etc;
- noting where children lack specified items of vocabulary, then including such items (preferably where they are meaning-related), in focused vocabulary sessions (e.g. dedicated to the language of music/cooking/sport);

- noting the pattern of code-switching in groups of children, so as to see whether it is motivated *socially* (who is in the group at the time?) or *linguistically* (is there evidence of vocabulary deficiency?);
- pitching language at a level slightly in advance of a child's current level of competence, by using more complex forms or controlled amounts of unknown vocabulary, so as to make linguistic demands on the learner;
- noting frequent pairings of children and managing them in such a way as to ensure bilinguals learners learn from suitable models (who may of course be bilingual themselves);
- engaging in one-to-one talk with bilingual children, paying special attention to the structuring of discourse, but equally making sure they direct the conversation to their own topics;
- being careful, in such conversations, to extend and develop children's utterances rather than to curtail them; to avoid 'forced-choice' questions or those that can be answered 'yes/no' or with a response constituted by a single bare noun.

As the above list shows, listening in to conversations is important. Similarly, putting children into different groups and settings to assess how they respond to and learn from different conversational partners is likely to pay dividends. There is evidence (for example, Tarone and Liu, 1995) that the partners with whom second language learners interact vitally influence the rate and route of their language development. Tarone and Liu showed that teachers seeking to simplify a task for learners – perhaps by asking questions which demand only a yes/no or one-word answer – actually deprive learners of opportunities to experiment with more complex structures. A skilful teacher can pitch questions at a level demanding suitable effort from learners, thus promoting language acquisition.

Developing an informal, shared system for recording children's language, too, will help. Individual teachers need to devise ways of recording their own evidence. For example, they might 'home in' on errors in the formation of plurals, past tenses, prepositions. Instances of where lexis has not been absorbed by bilingual children in the same way (for example, at the same rate) as by others are shown by Janes (2001) as crucial to the administration of the literacy hour. Further instances of successful communicative partnerships between monolinguals and bilinguals are distinguished by co-operative activity leading to fluent and purposeful talk. This evidence needs to be brought into discussions between teams of teachers (for example, a Year 1 team) as a possible basis for making decisions about progress, groupings, literacy and so on.

During such team discussions, teachers will be used to making distinctions between various languages – home language, 'mother tongue', additional language, and so on. These labels are convenient for 'off-the-cuff' discussion, but they may not correlate with how language actually operates in children's minds. Certainly, children from rich linguistic backgrounds with well-honed communicative skills are more likely to do well than not in school. Such children may come from any type of home, monolingual or bilingual. A school will succeed for them where it is well-informed about their homes, attends to parental expectations, notices what the children's language abilities are on entry and balances a language curriculum which suits them against due attention to the demands of a centralised curriculum. While such schools may have the know-how to resolve vocabulary difficulties (as we saw in the picture-story example above), we cannot claim all bilinguals are advantaged just because they enjoy an 'enhanced awareness of language' or are a 'linguistic resource' (Bhatt and Martin-Jones, 1992) the school can draw on. Too many reports over the last thirty years – Swann, Kingman, Cox – have reiterated such empty rhetoric supposing that there is a resource 'in there' but giving teachers no insight into how the resource can be accessed. Nor can we say that just because young children lack English on entering school, they have an educational disadvantage. A child's cognitive development (at least in the most favourable cases) may have taken place via their first language. A child who has progressed well in one language is likely to do so in another.

In conclusion, we should think less of 'languages' as variable codes, and more of 'language' as the educational constant. A 'top-down' approach to language teaching which assumes a diversity of individual codes must be balanced by a 'bottom-up' one, which sees children as potential communicators, able to make use of whatever language resources are available, and, when required, to operate within and across environments. It is the responsibility of teachers to see that the level of language used in classrooms is driven by real interchanges of meaning in cognitively demanding contexts. Then we can expect to see successful learning and reach further towards pedagogical excellence.

7. A Genre-Based Approach to the Teaching of Literacy

Melanie Bradley

Genre: commonplace – common meaning?

I first heard the term 'genre' applied to language and literacy learning in 1994. Although I had studied English before deciding to become a primary teacher, my understanding of the term was vague and it certainly had no impact on my work with children or students. It took the intervention of one of my colleagues, a linguist researching the nature of teachers' English subject knowledge, to enlighten me. It is significant that my colleague was a linguist. Back then, in Britain at least, 'genre theory' was very much the preserve of academics. It had begun to inform teaching methods in Australia and its effects were being debated in remote linguistic journals. For British primary teachers working to accommodate an evolving National Curriculum the concept of genre was as distant as the country in which it originated.

With the advent of the National Literacy Strategy (DfEE, 1998) things changed. Children had to be taught to read and write a range of 'text types', or genres. Training materials and in-service training had been devised with the aim of making the teaching of genres 'manageable', 'meaningful' and 'fun'. Thus, within a few years of the strategy's inception, genre became the fashionable buzzword in English pedagogy.

As a teacher educator, I now work with students whose initial teacher training in primary English has been dominated by the National Literacy Strategy and for whom the teaching of genres is an accepted norm. As developing teachers working in school, they have neither seen nor implemented any other English curriculum and feel no compunction to question its associated pedagogies. The two most commonly voiced concerns of the trainee teacher are 'what should I teach?' and 'how?' With reference to genre, the first question can be answered with relative ease. The National Literacy Strategy Framework for Teaching indicated that the requisite text types for primary aged children are:

- recount;
- narrative;
- report;
- instruction;
- persuasion;
- discussion;
- explanation.

Coverage must also be given to a range of poetic forms. The National Literacy Strategy is not, of course, a statutory curriculum but it would be a mistake to assume that the teaching of genres is similarly unenforceable. The National Curriculum for English – mandatory across the state sector – stipulates that children must write in 'a range of forms' (*c.f.* En3, 12, at Key Stage 1 and 2). No specification is given to the timing or organisation of teaching these forms as in the National Literacy Strategy, but the National Curriculum guidance notes state unambiguously:

> The programme of study for English and the National Literacy Strategy Framework for Teaching are closely related. The Framework provides a detailed basis for implementing the statutory requirements of the programmes of study for reading and writing. (DfEE/QCA, 2000: 20, 28)

The generic content laid down is thus, in effect, statutory.

Establishing *what* must be taught does not, of course, automatically resolve the question of *how* learning objectives can most effectively be met. There is now a burgeoning industry of manuals designed to give teachers structured lesson plans for addressing termly objectives across the National Literacy Strategy. Hence, when initial teacher training students prepare English schemes of work for teaching practice, it is becoming increasingly common for schools to request they adhere to a pre-determined sequence of published lessons in order to meet the literacy targets for which they will be responsible.

This is a development which should raise significant questions about the place of genre within the English curriculum and its implications for the nature of teaching and learning in language and literacy.

Of course, schools have long drawn on published resources, some of which contain imaginative and useful ideas to support the planning of busy practitioners. It is an accepted maxim, however, that schemes are only as good as the person who uses them. Differentiation, relevance, engagement and long-term progression can only be ensured if teachers' planning reflects knowledge of pupils as well as understanding of the nature and purpose of the learning objectives to be taught. Part of the process of becoming a successful teacher is learning to tailor an externally prescribed curriculum to the idiosyncratic interests, experiences and priorities of diverse classes of individual children. This creates a three-dimensional challenge: that teachers continue to evolve in their knowledge and understanding of discrete subjects; that they retain an enquiring approach to the nature of children's learning; and that they use this dynamic body of experience to interpret, manage and facilitate the mastery of given objectives by unique groups of pupils.

It is a process that is incompatible with an emerging culture of mass-targeted, manual-inspired literacy learning. Whilst there is no research evidence to suggest that this culture is widespread, the fact that it should exist at all suggests a lack of confidence and common understanding amongst practitioners with regard to their interpretation and implementation of the National Literacy Strategy. If this is so, then the question of how genres might effectively be taught cannot be addressed before it is established why we now have what might be termed a genre-based English curriculum.

Why genre?

During the 1990s concern about literacy standards had become increasingly focused on pupils' ability to read and reproduce in writing a range of textual forms. After a period of intense debate on the teaching of reading which peaked in response to the work of Turner (1991), attention was gradually repositioned to address the pedagogy of writing. A common theme, which was to span the 1990s, emerged in a DES report of 1992:

> room for further improvement remains; much of the required writing was of stories ... and there were few opportunities for other kinds of writing. (14)

It was a concern which would not easily be laid to rest. A survey of teachers' views on literacy learning conducted by Lewis and Wray (1995) revealed that, whilst over 95 per cent 'agreed strongly' that 'children need to write for a range of audiences and in a range of styles in order to become effective writers', their discussion of writing pedagogy focused heavily on the production of narrative texts. Only 15 per cent of teachers referred to the writing of non-fiction and, of the 55 per cent who mentioned the need to introduce children to 'a range of texts', their suggested range was limited primarily to 'fiction' texts, namely 'poetry and *different types of story*' (original italics).

Just prior to the introduction of the National Literacy Strategy in schools, a QCA (1998a: 15) analysis of Key Stage 1 SATs results reported that:

> Pupils still prefer to write narrative but show little progress in their use and range of narrative conventions ... The structure and organisation of pupils' non-narrative writing is less secure than that of narrative.

For those anticipating development in writing trends across the primary phase, the official findings of standards at Key Stage 2 (QCA, 1998b: 16) were bleakly familiar:

> Pupils still prefer to write narrative but show little progress in their use and range of narrative conventions ... The structure and organisation of pupils' non-narrative writing is less secure than that of narrative.

By the end of the first year of the National Literacy Strategy in schools, OFSTED (1999: 11, 15, 16) reported a similar lack of generic variety and attention to textual form in the teaching of writing:

> Very few lessons were observed in which pupils' writing skills were developed in a planned, sustained and challenging way; too often the outcomes took the form of lists of words ... [while] few teachers used non-fiction texts as the model for pupils' writing ... [and only in a] small proportion of lessons [did work focus on] the specific features of a genre.

In short, as the twentieth century drew to a close, the most commonly taught genre in primary schools was narrative, which had been given priority to the detriment of other text types. The bewildering irony was that, despite this generic imbalance, pupils were still tending to organise and express their written narratives ineffectually.

There is no reason to doubt the veracity of these findings, but their constancy in the face of repeated official censure raises important questions about the sort of conditions necessary to bring about fundamental change in primary English pedagogy. The feasibility of change would seem to depend most obviously on the development of teachers' English subject knowledge. Before decisions can be taken about the specific nature of requisite subject knowledge, however, it is important to consider the more general issue of motivational factors underpinning change in the primary teacher.

Research into the 'psychology' of primary teachers suggests that, however much they may appear to subscribe to the necessity of collegial or whole-school practices, their main priority and source of job satisfaction is working to support pupils' development within the essentially private world of their own classrooms (Nias *et al.*, 1989; Duncan, 1999). A related difficulty inherent in the job of class teachers is that they tend only to work with individual children – albeit intensively – for a year. Hence, despite the prevalence of detailed record keeping and assessment procedures, whole school planning and statutory curricula, they do not directly oversee the process of pupil development in any learning area. Yet such a long-term perspective is arguably essential if the challenge of facilitating genuine progression across the primary phase is to be appreciated and addressed. This is a view which the case study below would appear to support.

Generic development or regression?
One child's experience of Narrative Learning between Key Stage 1 and 2

In 1991 Lisa, aged 6, wrote the following narrative entitled "The Time Machine" (Figure 7.1). An enthusiastic writer with a strong sense of authorship, she arrived in school one Monday morning with 'a new book I've made', happily anticipating the ritual of 'author's time' in which she would share her writing with the rest of the class as they assumed the role of critical audience. How should one begin to assess it?

There are many linguistic and structural criteria by which narratives may be judged. Increasingly over the past thirty years, research has highlighted the cognitive, social and emotional, as well as linguistic and literacy gains which may be made by the young child through the medium of the story. The process of listening to stories read aloud and told verbally appears to reinforce narrative conventions, embed new vocabulary and help the child to

Ones There was
a Man who had
a timew MACHINE
and wanted to test
it.

Page 1

a puff ok smok
opperd onsome
Brit colors

Page 2

(40 millyen Years)
thene he was In the
Past and saw Dinebohrs
he said I most writ
this Down in my Book
So he Did.

Page 3

But I forst so
he was Reting
his Book the
Dinosor
Saelu wats tht ter.
The man sask
is my book.

Page 4

So the Dinoseps
never were Bovered
a gayn.

Page 5

Cut the
Dinospididet
Eat the man and
the time
mAchine so the
man Got in the
timemAchine and
PULLed The Lever
and whent to Rast
The

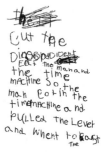

Page 6

Page 7

So he waved
to all the
boys inthe
cimny and
went to have
some breade
and went
back to his time machine

the
~~the boot~~
he pressed some more buttons
and pulled the leaver and found
himself in the 22nd century

Page 8

So he got out
of his time machine
and this is wat
he saw.

Page 9

He got back in to his
time machine and pressed his
buttons for a hundred
years later and when the
time machine stopped what
he saw scared him very
much because there was
no earth man had killed
it. All that was left was
a ball of fire.

Page 10

So it took four
owers to get
back and he
all-ways had
his adventures
onthe time machine

Page 11

The
End

Page 12

Figure 7.1:　The Time Machine

assimilate the distinctive patterns and structures of written language (Wells, 1987). There is a strong body of support for Hardy's (1968) seminal comment that narrative is a 'primary act of mind' (for example, Chukovsky, 1963; Moffett, 1968; Gregory, 1974; Paley, 1981; Whitehead, 1997). In assessing Lisa's story, therefore, it is helpful to weigh it against Chambers' (1985: 5) criterion that successful literature gives the reader 'images to think with'. Lisa wrote her story at home 'in bursts' over the course of a weekend, a fact that is probably reflected in the fragmented and varied quality of her composition. She wrote it independently, only at one point asking her mother to add her dictated amendments when she 'wanted to change a bit but couldn't squeeze it in,' (see page 8 in her narrative).

It is possible to suggest a number of areas in which Lisa's conceptual understanding of narrative form and her linguistic capability might be developed. (I shall omit reference to transcriptional weaknesses as my assessment focus here is purely generic.) Although she begins the story with a basic orientation on page 1, no sense of characterisation is evoked and for much of the narrative there is little attention to place. There are points at which narrative coherence breaks down and sentences have no obvious causal link with preceding or subsequent text, for example 'So the dinosaurs never were bovered again' (page 5) and 'But the dinosaurs didn't eat the man …' (page 6). There are also cohesive weaknesses. For instance, there is an example of syntactic confusion, 'But the dinosaur didn't eat the man and the time machine …' (page 6), while connectives are limited to the oft-repeated 'but', 'and', 'so' and 'then'. The narrative ends abruptly with no sense of thematic resolution or structural completion.

Given these more salient undeveloped features, "The Time Machine" perhaps evinces only a tenuous adherence to Knapp and Watkins' (1994: 22) definition of narration as a process which 'sequences people and events in time and space'. If, however, one applies Chambers' criterion to page 10 of the story, the qualitative assessment alters significantly:

> He got back in to his time machine and pressed his buttons for a hundred years later and when the time machine stopped what he saw scared him very much because there was no Earth. Man had killed it. All that was left was a ball of fire.

Why there is such a radical development in Lisa's narrative skill in this brief passage it is impossible to say. Although we had discussed conservation issues in class and read Michael Foreman's splendid fable about or shared concern for the natural world, *Dinosaurs and all that Rubbish* (1972), there is no evidence of plagiarism from this or any other text. Moreover, she received no compositional assistance at any stage of the writing process. In this brief passage, however, Lisa succeeds through her control of sentence construction in creating a simple, yet starkly effective, apocalyptic vision. She has given the reader a single, powerful image to stimulate pause for thought and, in so doing, indicated a potential for narrative writing which had yet to be tapped.

Five years later, as she was about to enter Year 6 Lisa produced "The Magic Book" (see example in Figure 7.2). Whilst it is unreliable to assess writing skills on one sample, this text nevertheless provokes important questions about what constitutes narrative progression and how generic development is to be ensured across the primary phase. It is really not possible to identify anything other than the most superficial points of narrative progression in this text. If characterisation was ignored in "The Time Machine", it is conveyed only incidentally here through basic authorial comment (for example, 'Holly thought he was a pest ...' page 1) and surface dialogue. Scene setting is perfunctory and no appreciable sense of time is conveyed, rendering the orientation of the reader barely more skilful than in the earlier work. The syntactic confusion prevalent in "The Time Machine" has disappeared, but sentence construction remains significantly under-developed, lacking in variety or complexity. Reporting clauses are noticeably repetitious and there are occasional lapses into non-standard English. There is no use of paragraphing to mark structural development. At no stage in the text is the reader stimulated to wonder or reflect on events.

What, then, can be learned from the work of this one child? If Chambers was correct in his assertion that the successful narrator gives the reader 'images to think with' then, in this very important respect, Lisa might be said to have *regressed* between Key Stage 1 and 2. This is not, however, simply because the earlier tale touches on the theme of global annihilation which arguably holds more *gravitas* than a fantasy outing. Stories can legitimately serve a wide variety of purposes and their success is determined less by theme than by the extent to which a particular purpose has been realized by the author. It should be stressed that this is *not* a cosy, relativistic approach to the assessment of writing. The logical conclusion to such an approach would be to judge *Gone with the Wind* as being equal to *Anna Karenina* simply because each involves a love affair and has greatly satisfied its respective readership. Beyond sharing romantic elements there is not the remotest parallel of linguistic, thematic or universal magnitude between these two stories.

Page 1

The Magic book

Holly was 10 years old. She had a younger brother called Scott who was 4 years old. He couldn't really say things properly. Holly thought he was a pest. One day Holly's mother said to her "Holly, take your brother to the park over the road." "Yes mum" said Holly. "And be sure your back at 1.00" "Yes mum" said Holly. Holly took her brothers hand and they went to the park. When they got there Holly sat down on a bench while her brother played football with his friend from over the road. There wasn't anything to do over the park. There were baby swings and a small slide and that was it. Scott thought the slide was great fun. But Holly was bored. "I'm just going to have a quick walk around the park" she said. "I won't be too long" "Alright" said Scott. She walked over to the trees. It was a bit like a forest with trees and a little lake running through them. She walked further and further until finally she was lost. "Oh no" she said. "I'm lost" She started to cry. Then she herd a rustling in the trees. A man jumped out of the leaves and looked at her. He looked very strange. He had bright green eyes and pointed ears. "Who are you" he said "I'm Holly" she

Page 2

said wiping away her tears. "Who are you?" "I'm woodly" said the man. "I look after all the forests / jungley and the animals in them all over the world". "It must be very hard keeping an eye on all of them if they are all over the world" said Holly. "Oh no, itt quite easy" The man said. He put his hand in onto his pocket and pulled out a small book. It was green with no pictures on the front. It had no title either. "This book has pictures of all the forests and animals from all over the world." "When I put my finger on one of the pictures and say go I end up in that place. If I want to go back home I say home and I'm back in my forest". "Wow" I said Holly. "I have 2 of these books in case I loose one of them" said the man. "You may have one if you like" "Yes please" said Holly. The man passed the book toher. "I have to go n" said the man. He opened his book and flicked through the pages. He stopped at a picture of a rabbit. "Go" He said and he vanished. Holly started to walk back the way she came and finally came back to were her brother was playing football "Come on scott" said Holly hiding the book behind her back. "It's just gone 1.00" The went back home. When they got thierb Holly went up to her room and sat down on her bed. She turned the pages carefully. She came to a picture of

Page 3

a lion "go" she shouted. Suddenly she found her self sitting on a rock with bushes around her. She pushed the leaves of the bushes aside and saw lots of lions lying in the sun!

Then a great big male lion started to walk towards her. "Home"! She shouted an she was sitting on herbed. She had many, many, adventures with this magic book yet still managed to keep it a secret. One day she went on an adventure to see how elephants lived for a project at school. She kept her book for many many years. When she was old she puit it in a box and buried it in the ground. People look for that book and today they still cant find it.

The end

Figure 7.2:   The Magic Book

"The Time Machine" and "The Magic Book" *are*, however, essentially the same *type* of narrative – a simple fantasy adventure – and are intended to serve the same *function*, that of inviting the reader to feel vicariously the experiences of the main character. Their success, therefore, depends on whether we are engaged, thrilled and stirred to imagine by the sights and events to which we are exposed. This only happens once to any significant degree in "The Time Machine" because of the way in which language has been manipulated to convey the apocalyptic scene. If we have been given no images to transport us into a fantasy world in "The Magic Book", this is then directly attributable to the author's failure to apply the structural and linguistic tools of the narrative genre.

It must be asked why Lisa was apparently unable by the end of the primary phase to capitalise on the signs of narrative potential that were discernible near the start of her formal education. Speculation is obviously unreliable, particularly when her learning experiences between the ages of six and eleven are unknown. It is not altogether unreasonable, however, to guess at a likely scenario. Unless Lisa had been taught by English specialists – a likely minority amongst primary teachers whose overall, cross-curricular knowledge is bound to be generalised – how could they have *known* what constitutes narrative progression? In the absence of such knowledge, it would still have been quite feasible for the dedicated class teacher to be satisfied that Lisa had developed as a story writer. Why? Because, regardless of whether her linguistic limitations had been recognised, at least she was writing at far greater *length* than she had done at Key Stage 1.

If it is so difficult to ensure progression in the most commonly taught genre of all, how can the typical generalist primary teacher be expected to teach the other six text types of the National Literacy Strategy with any greater measure of understanding or success? Achieving generic development would seem logically to depend on teachers understanding not only the distinctive purposes and linguistic characteristics of any given text type, but also what constitutes reasonable evidence of progression in the composition of each genre at different stages across the primary phase.

When, in 1994, this problem was first drawn to my attention, there was no official recognition of the issue nor any likelihood of imminent remedial action at national level. If I wanted to discover more about the feasibility of developing teachers', and thereby children's, English subject knowledge, then I would have to turn to the country which at that time, more than any other, had addressed the matter head-on: Australia, the breeding ground for genre theory.

Developing knowledge about language in Britain and Australia: common dilemma – different response

There are many parallels between the teaching of English in Britain and Australia. By the late 1960s, both countries had abandoned the product-focused writing pedagogies of the past to embrace a more 'free' and 'creative' approach to compositional development. It had been recognised that formally learning the 'rules of English' had, for many children, resulted in confusion and disaffection with the act of writing. In particular, the common method of teaching grammatical and punctuation concepts through de-contextualised exercises had often failed to give children an understanding of their function within texts. Hence, although a child might have been able to locate action verbs within a given passage and recite that 'an action verb is a verb which denotes physical action,' he or she would not necessarily have recognised that suspense passages within narratives are typically characterised by a pre-dominance of these verbs.

Across the 1960s and 1970s, a 'personal growth' view of language learning, was much in vogue in both countries. This is perhaps best conveyed by the 'dead pigeon in the playground' scenario – that is, deceased winged creature is discovered by children on the way in to school, appealing strongly to the more gruesome natural instincts of the typical primary-aged child. Their class teacher, recognising this as an exciting, first-hand stimulus for purposeful writing, takes the children outside to examine the corpse and speculate on the likely cause of its sad demise. The morning's original activity has been abandoned but the children have replaced it with a self-initiated learning experience imbued with personal significance.

As Medway (1990: 23) observed, the overriding emphasis at this time was on 'the importance of response and spontaneity' in 'creative' writing in order to develop 'growth' in pupils. This view is supported by a contemporary report by a team of American observers which stated that: 'The teaching of English in British schools is the teaching of creative response. Involvement in the creative act seems to be the primary goal ... Feeling and doing, not knowing, are the critical concerns ...' (Squire and Applebee, 1969: 218).

By the 1980s, the 'psycholinguistic' movement, which was championed by researchers such as Kenneth and Yetta Goodman, Donald Graves and Frank Smith, was advocating a 'whole language' or *process*-based approach to literacy learning. Summarised crudely, this approach drew an analogy between the process of learning to speak and that of literacy development. It was proposed that, if the acquisition of speech occurs naturally and young children are able to make active sense of grammatical constructions without any formal instruction, then a similar process – one which stresses the inter-relationship between thought and language – should be possible with the learning of reading and writing. Teachers in Britain and Australia were urged to learn from the way in which parents interact with infants to facili-tate language-learning: developing speech within meaningful contexts, inter-preting and providing words where necessary but eschewing formal training techniques. (Indeed, where rote correction was used, this was generally found to be counter-productive, as children appeared to assimilate the rules of grammar over time, at first generalising, then actively refining their under-standing of grammatical irregularities with experience.) The assumption was that, given appropriate support within meaningful contexts, young children, who generally come to school with considerable *innate* knowledge of written language, could reasonably be expected to undergo the *emergence* of actual literacy skills. 'Naturalistic', 'emergent' or 'process-orientated' literacy peda-gogies undoubtedly had some positive effects in Britain and Australia. It was found that, encouraged to understand the complete writing process from initial draft to final transcription and also viewing themselves as authors communicating with real audiences, children tended to experience a greater sense of purpose in, and ownership over, writing activities.

Alas, not all of the effects were so positive. By the late 1980s researchers on both sides of the world had identified four significant issues arising from naturalistic literacy pedagogies.

(1) In Australia, as in Britain, it was being recognised that, whilst the use of personal recount and narrative was important for children, an over-emphasis on these text types was significantly limiting their cognitive and communicative potential. As Donaldson (1989: 25) argued: 'They need to learn gradually over the school years, how to participate in the impersonal modes of thinking and linguistic expression that are such an important part of our cultural heritage.'

(2) Opinion was shifting to suggest that, whilst there are significant parallels between the processes of acquiring oral language and literacy skills, a complete analogy is unrealistic. Donaldson (1989) contended that, whilst it is essential to develop reading and writing skills in meaningful contexts using language that reflects natural speech patterns, most children will require *structured adult intervention*

to ensure the acquisition of literacy concepts. This is because, in the absence of the facial, gestural, intonational and concrete support received by the emerging speaker, children beginning to decode or encode text face a much more abstract challenge.

(3) If literacy standards were to improve, then, children clearly needed to acquire a more *conscious* understanding of *how* and *why* texts are constructed. Teaching methods which made these linguistic concepts *explicit* were required.

(4) Unfortunately, by the late 1980s, British and Australian schools were largely staffed by a generation of teachers who themselves had never received any explicit linguistic education.

Hence, the common challenge for both countries lay in deciding:

- the nature of English subject knowledge required by pupils *and* their teachers; and
- a pedagogy which would ensure effective development of linguistic and literacy concepts in ways that would be relevant and meaningful to young learners.

In Britain, the politically sensitive nature of the English language would ensure that these issues would continue to be the subject of fierce debate until the inception of the National Literacy Strategy. The Kingman Report (1988), which advocated developing grammatical competence within a socio-linguistic context, had been officially rejected since it did not deliver a return to the formal transmission of Latinate grammar the government desired. For its similar failure to unite formal grammar teaching with explorations of language usage, teaching materials arising from the Language in the National Curriculum Project (DES, 1990) were never released for publication in primary schools. Australia had no comparable obstacles to what was regarded as a national priority and would address the issue of language and literacy development by embracing a radical new pedagogy.

Genre theory: the way forward?

Genre-based approaches to the teaching of literacy have derived from the linguistic theory of Michael Halliday. According to Halliday (1973), all language use is essentially a *functional* enterprise. In other words, we learn to *listen, speak, think, read* and *write* in a variety of ways to help us achieve a range of practical ends.

As babies we acquire language to communicate our needs, form relationships and understand more about the world around us. As we develop, we refine our use of language in order to enhance our communicative, social and cognitive skills. Thus, as we mature linguistically, we increase our ability to function effectively in society. In the young or linguistically immature, knowledge about language use is largely *implicit*, thus limiting their capacity as functioning social beings. The logical extension of this view is that only if we *consciously* learn about language can we more fully exploit its infinite potential.

For Halliday, social behaviour and language use are inextricably linked. He argued (1973) that all human activities give rise to the creation of texts, be they *mental, spoken or written.* Because all texts are created within a social context they are shaped in response to a specific audience and purpose. Different social situations are naturally characterised by particular modes of behaviour and discourse (or text):

> What is common to every use of language is that it is meaningful, contextualised and in the broadest sense social ... The child is surrounded by language, but not in the form of grammars and dictionaries, or of randomly chosen words and sentences, or of undirected monologue. What he encounters is 'text' or language in use; sequences of language articulated each within itself and with the situation in which it occurs ... The child's awareness of language cannot be isolated from his awareness of language function, and this conceptual unity offers a useful vantage point from which language may be seen in a perspective that is educationally relevant. (20)

Indeed, by the 1980s researchers including Frances Christie, Gunther Kress, J.R. Martin and Joan Rothery had embraced Halliday's theory to inform the development of a new literacy pedagogy. These genre theorists argued that when a social situation recurs frequently, such as a tabloid news report or a medical consultation, the resultant text types become so familiar to us in terms of structure, grammar and style that they may be said to represent particular genres (Kress, 1987).

Consider the following two examples of a medical consultation:

Scenario 1

Doctor: Good morning, do take a seat.
Patient: Thank you, Doctor.
Doctor: Now, what seems to be the trouble?
Patient: Well, I've had a sore throat for the past fortnight so I thought
           I'd better have it checked out.
Doctor: Right, if you'll just open wide, I'll take a look.

Scenario 2

Doctor: Hiya! Take a pew.
Patient: Thanks, Doc.
Doctor: So what's the story?
Patient: Well, my throat's been giving me gip for the past fortnight so
           I thought I'd better see the quack.
Doctor: Open up the old laughing gear, then, and I'll take a butchers.

The doctor-patient consultation is so commonplace that few people would have any difficulty in recognising that the vocabulary and register used within the second scenario are wholly at odds with the accepted linguistic conventions for this particular social interaction. We implicitly *know* the rules of the genre. This is not true of all social contexts, however. Moreover, when language takes the form of writing, which has significantly different features from speech, recognising and applying the rules of discourse are, for many people, far from natural.

Genre theorists contend that certain written genres (for example, explanation or argument) have particular social currency because of the important communicative functions they enable the writer to fulfil; without mastering these, pupils will be disadvantaged. Because children come to school from diverse social backgrounds, it is necessary to make the characteristics of these genres maximally explicit for all. Genre theorists consider this a matter of social equity. Kress (1987: 43) perhaps best sums up their aspiration when he stated: 'As a minimal goal I would wish every writer to have access to all powerful genres.'

A genre-based approach to the teaching of literacy is thus intended to help children to *communicate* to a range of *audiences* for a range of *purposes* using different types of *text*. Viewed from this perspective learning about genres is, in effect, learning how to *mean*.

Genre theory in practice

It should be stressed that support for genre theory in Australia is far from unanimous. It has been interpreted in a variety of ways and with widely differing levels of success across the country. In particular, where pedagogy fails to respect the social and functional dimensions of language learning, fundamental problems have been found to emerge.

As Dixon (1987) argued, most texts, being multi-purpose, are also multi-generic. A letter of complaint, for example, would probably incorporate explanatory and reporting elements within what is essentially an argument. Thus, it is pedagogically and linguistically unsound to recommend formulaic generic models to teachers. In the worst case scenarios genre-based pedagogy has become a 'teaching by numbers' exercise precluding individual creativity and conceptual development. Ironically, pupils exposed to methodologies of this kind have subsequently failed to learn through or about language, the fundamental aim of genre theory.

In Western Australia Knapp and Watkins (1994) devised a teaching approach aimed at addressing these problems. Firstly they differentiated between 'genre' and 'text type', arguing that, although in one sense these terms can refer to a single text, 'there are clear distinctions in the ways they name and classify the text'. Knapp and Watkins suggested that in school-based writing there are five key genres: *describing, explaining, instructing, arguing* and *narrating.* They refer to *text types* as the *products* of these genres (see Figure 7.3). Hence, the narrative genre may include products ranging from simple personal recounts to ancient fables exploring universal themes. They would agree with Dixon that many text types are multi-generic, but do not recognise this as problematic provided that teachers maintain social function as the guiding criterion for any decisions relating to a text's structural or grammatical features. The following text is given to exemplify their position.

> Ants are tiny and quick insects. An ant is black and red. It moves fast. It lays eggs. A queen ant has wings. Ants collect food from the ground. An ant has six legs, two antennas and three body parts. (11)

Although the primary function (that is, genre) of this text is *describing*, the type of description (that is, text type) is a *report*. Incontestable facts are being described to inform us of what *is*. There is no need to evoke a subjective

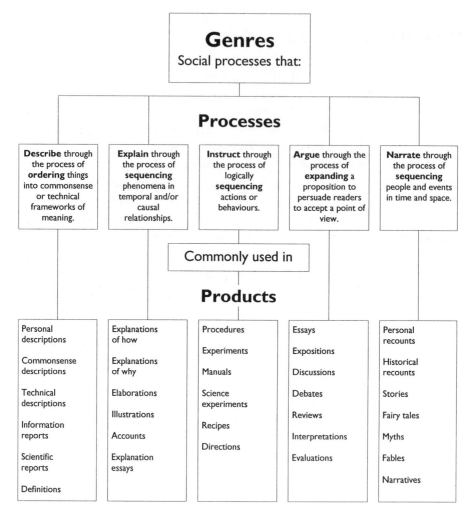

Figure 7.3:   Text types (Knapp and Watkins, 1994)

response in the reader. Hence the description is suitably unadorned, objective and expressed in the present tense. This contrasts strongly with the sort of personal description that may be used to introduce characters in a narrative. Consider, for example, the introduction to William Beech in *Goodnight Mister Tom* (Magorian, 1981)

> The boy was thin and sickly-looking, pale with limp sandy hair and dull grey eyes.

The emotive quality of the physical details described here hints at the child's health and psychological state. Moved by his apparent vulnerability the reader begins to speculate about William's past. These effects are further enhanced by juxtaposing references to William and Mister Tom:

> Although he was of average height, in Willie's eyes he was a towering giant with skin like coarse, wrinkled brown paper and a voice like thunder.

Beyond the obvious use of contrast, the child-like use of simile ensures that we view Mister Tom from Willie's perspective and appreciate his sense of awe for the old man. As the author intends, the *nature* of the description has caused us to imagine, infer and empathise.

Although the scientific report and narrative extracts above are both essentially describing, their different social functions have been fulfilled by quite distinct use of grammatical and structural features. It is useful to consider how Knapp and Watkins (1994: 148-50) put their process model of genre teaching into practice.

One of the most commonly found and, for generations of children, much reviled writing tasks in primary classrooms is 'Weekend News'. It is not uncommon to find disaffected pupils regurgitating the same events each Monday morning and making little discernible progression in the quality of their writing. This may well relate to the fact that many weekends follow a fairly similar pattern which gives children little stimulus to compose. It must also be asked, however, to what extent pupils consciously understand the function or linguistic characteristics of this particular text type.

In the following genre-based approach to 'Weekend News', Knapp and Watkins sought to unite context, text and grammar. According to their process model, 'Weekend News' is an example of the personal recount text, a product of the narrative genre. The lesson is aimed at Year 4 but could quite easily be modified for younger pupils by extending the time spent on teacher modelling and shared composition:

> The lesson begins in a shared writing context. The teacher asks for a volunteer to call out some significant happenings from the weekend. The class is then asked to re-tell the events and these are scribed chronologically by their teacher.

What Ryan did at the weekend

- went trampolining;
- did some stretches;
- put socks on;
- warmed up;
- practised routine;
- bell rang;
- started routine;
- passed a level;
- Mum bought him a badge.

The teacher explains how each of these activities involved something *happening* and that the word describing the happening is called an 'action verb'. The class is next asked to identify each of the action verbs in Ryan's news list as the teacher underlines these for emphasis.

- <u>went</u> trampolining;
- <u>did</u> some stretches;
- <u>put</u> socks on;
- <u>warmed</u> up;
- <u>practised</u> routine;
- bell <u>rang</u>;
- <u>started</u> routine;
- <u>passed</u> a level;
- Mum <u>bought</u> him a badge.

The teacher may choose at this point to discuss how and why tenses are used, asking the pupils to explain why the action verbs they have identified are in the past tense.

The teacher explains that special words or phrases are needed to link and sequence these different events. According to the developmental stage of the children, examples of temporal, causal and additive conjunctions may be analysed explicitly to consider their function in connecting pieces of information – 'phrases and clauses'. Attention is then re-focused on the list of things Ryan did at the weekend and the class is asked to suggest conjunctions that might be used to link the events together. They may be further challenged to identify the types of conjunction they have suggested.

The list of conjunctions is left on the board and pupils are asked to refer to this as they write a *recount* of Ryan's weekend. It would, of course, be quite feasible for this independent work to be preceded by writing modelled by the teacher or shared composition.

A text prepared by the teacher or written by one of the children is then displayed for shared analysis of its grammatical features. The class is asked to identify the action verbs (underlined) and the conjunctions (double-underlined).

> On Saturday Ryan <u>went</u> trampolining at Ryde. <u>When</u> he <u>got</u> there he <u>did</u> some stretches <u>and</u> <u>put</u> his socks on. <u>Shortly after that</u> he <u>warmed up</u> <u>and</u> <u>practised</u> his routine. Time <u>passed</u>, the bell <u>rang</u> <u>and</u> he <u>started</u>. <u>After</u> his routine Ryan <u>passed</u> level four <u>and</u> his mum <u>bought</u> him a badge. Ryan was glad he <u>passed</u>.

The grid format below is used to consolidate understanding of the main grammatical features of the recount.

Action verbs	Conjunctions
Went	when
got	and
did	shortly after that
put	and
warmed up	and
practised	after
passed	and
started	
bought	

Pupils may then apply this analysis independently to their own recounts. Where the teacher believes additional support is required the activities remain shared.

The *structural* features of the recount genre must next be made explicit. The teacher explains that recounts typically have:

(1) an orientation stage which introduces the reader to key people, time and place;

(2) a sequence of related events;

(3) an optional evaluation which generally involves a basic interpretation of the main events of the recount by the writer.

Pupils are asked to identify these stages in the text they have analysed together during shared reading.

On Saturday Ryan went trampolining at Ryde	Orientation
When he got there he did some stretches and put his socks on. Shortly after that he warmed up and practised his routine. Time passed, the bell rang and he was ready to go. After his routine Ryan passed level four and his mum bought him a badge.	Sequence of events
Ryan was glad he passed.	Evaluation

When sufficiently confident, pupils may apply this structure to their own, independently produced recounts.

Reading and writing: the critical link

Although any discussion of genre-based pedagogies inevitably focuses on writing, it should be stressed that conceptual understanding of, and literary competence in, any genre is dependent on critical reading of generic text types. It is only through shared reading with a linguistically knowledgeable teacher that pupils will begin to identify the grammatical and structural features of a text type and relate these to social function. The ultimate aim, given the infinite variety of text types they may encounter in life, is that pupils will develop into independent critical readers. During the primary phase, however, independent reading and writing must be continually reinforced through teacher-supported analysis of skills and concepts.

Knapp and Watkins (1994: 26) made three practical suggestions for critical reading:

(1) Texts chosen by teachers should be 'generically simple', as those which are unclear in their purpose and form provide poor models for pupils' own writing.

(2) Teachers should 'use the text as an object that can be pulled apart and examined'. In other words, pupils should be helped to analyse distinct elements of a text – their function and related structural/ grammatical features. For example, action sequences may typically have (i) a high proportion of action verbs (double-underlined below); (ii) sentences which become increasingly short as tension rises (italicised below) and (iii) action verbs used metaphorically to evoke effective imagery (underlined below). These features may be explored with pupils through analysis of brief passages as in the following example:

> Joe <u>ran</u> blindly through the woods, crying and gasping for breath. Suddenly, he <u>tripped</u> and <u>fell</u>. *The game was up.* In an instant the gang <u>pounced</u>. *Panic. Fear. Dread.* <u>His mind was gripped with all three. Insults raged above him</u>. *He was trapped.*

(3) Text types should be analysed over several readings, during which distinct aspects may be examined. It is counter-productive to explore too many generic features simultaneously. Key foci should include:

(i) purpose – what is the text trying to achieve?
(ii) message – what is the text about?
(iii) structure – what 'jobs' are different parts of the text designed to fulfil and (iv) grammar – what sort of language is being used to carry out each job?

The impact of genre theory on the National Literacy Strategy: a guarantee of excellence?

This strategy is Britain's most prescriptive English curriculum to date. Its specificity is directly related to its aim of raising pupils' conscious mastery of literacy skills, concepts and knowledge. With its emphasis on 'text types', 'shared' and 'modelled' work, the National Literacy Strategy may also – albeit loosely – be termed Britain's first genre-based English curriculum. This has significant implications for the development of English subject knowledge within the profession. The success of genre-based pedagogies would seem to be determined by teachers' understanding and interpretation of functional linguistic theory. Sadly, the speed with which the strategy was disseminated in primary schools and the delayed publication of its rationale (Beard, 1999) suggest a concern for implementation over understanding that militates against any notion of 'excellence' in English pedagogy. The rationale contains only two brief references to genre theory and a perfunctory, unrelated reference to Halliday later in the rationale. A functional model of language learning is neither discussed nor related to National Literacy Strategy content or pedagogy.

By definition, the strategy is concerned with the development of reading and writing but what of speaking and listening? Although we live in an increasingly print rich society, oral language arguably remains our primary tool for functional living. Research has shown that specific attention to oral development promotes conscious knowledge about language, its structures and functions and should thus be seen as integral to the acquisition of literacy skills, concepts and knowledge (Barnes, 1976; Barnes and Sheeran, 1992; Wells, 1987; 1992). Such a view is actually acknowledged in the National Literacy Strategy Framework for Teaching (DfEE, 1998: 3).

> Good oral work enhances pupils' understanding of language in both oral and written forms and of the way language can be used to communicate. It is also an important part of the process through which pupils read and compose texts.

This would seem self-evident. How, for example, could study of characterisation techniques within a narrative text not be enhanced by a drama activity designed to deepen pupils' understanding of a character's psychology? The programme of study for speaking and listening in the National Curriculum for English is, of course, statutory. Given the possibility that the National Literacy Strategy may be viewed now by many primary teachers as the official English curriculum, the current status of oracy – and thus the promotion of excellence – within language and literacy learning must be open to question.

The National Literacy Strategy may incorporate a broad range of text types but it makes no clear distinction between 'text type' and 'genre'. For example, the framework for teaching (DfEE, 1998) stipulates that pupils must study a wide variety of narrative texts – 'myths', 'legends', 'fables', 'fairytales', 'stories' and 'recounts'. Whilst it is desirable that pupils experience a broad literary range, the strategy does not make clear that these text types are all products of the narrative genre. As such they each exemplify the process of sequencing people and events in time and place whilst being differently shaped by their intended audience and purpose.

Another classic example of this confusion is that of the oft-repeated 'letter-writing genre' in primary classrooms. Of course, no such genre exists. Pupils must learn that every letter they write should draw uniquely on the characteristics of the main genres according to the unique social function it is intended to fulfil.

Unless this distinction between text type and genre is understood by teachers, it may be difficult for them to plan for sufficient recursive exploration of the main genres as discrete social processes. For their pupils, this will inevitably strengthen the challenge of flexibly and appropriately applying generic features to the texts they create.

Earlier in this chapter consideration was given to Knapp and Watkins' (1994) 'process' approach to the teaching of genres. The 'recount' lessons described are arguably well-structured, closely related to pupils' own experiences and linguistically sound. It cannot be denied, however, that recount is probably one of the most straightforward text types to teach. Its purpose, and hence its structural and grammatical features, tend to be fairly uncomplicated. Where texts have multiple functions and are multi-generic, however, the demands on teachers for flexible and imaginative application of advanced linguistic knowledge increase significantly. There is currently no adequate research available to assess the quality of teachers' response to this challenge. It would not seem unreasonable, however, to speculate that those lacking sufficient subject knowledge might resort to formulaic teaching models. Excessive use of writing frames, resulting in an over-simplification of textual features and encouraging dependency on the part of young writers, is an obvious manifestation of this dilemma. Another is teacher reliance on published lesson plans to fulfil National Literacy Strategy objectives. This gives rise to a further, key consideration – that of pupil motivation. As C. Rosen and H. Rosen (1973: 85) observed:

> It is easy to think of many reasons why a young child should not want to write and very difficult to think of reasons why he should. Even more baffling is the problem of what a young child thinks he is doing when he is writing, other than submitting to the will of adults …

It is perhaps inevitable that with the imposition of a radical new curriculum and pedagogy, teachers may grow increasingly distanced from the philosophy and practices associated with 'naturalistic' approaches to literacy learning. Complete polarisation of past and present methodologies is, however, rarely wise. At its best, the teaching of writing in the 1980s at least gave pupils a strong sense of audience, purpose and personal motivation fuelled by the prevailing notion of 'authorship'. As Hall and Robinson (1994: 6) argued:

> It is no accident that 'author' and 'authority' are related terms. Children who 'own' their texts will write meaningfully and will want to use their skills purposefully.

It should not be inferred from this that all happily motivated children will naturally become competent writers without skilful intervention; we know this is not the case. It does, however, raise the important question of pupils' perception, and hence *understanding*, of the writing process.

Consider the following text, independently written by James, aged 7 (Figure 7.4). The writing emerged naturally as he played with a friend who had come to stay for the night whilst their parents had a dinner party downstairs. The two boys decided to sabotage the meal and the writing records their plans for attack. The final page, beginning 'things to be aware of', was written after a cautionary warning from James' father. It is not very legible as it was written, not for an adult audience, but to assist the boys in their subterfuge. Accordingly, they crossed out each step as it was achieved and signalled their success with 'mission complete!' scrawled across page 1. The text is an example of the 'procedural' or 'instructional' genre and, despite the transcriptional errors one might expect in a play context, it successfully incorporates the main structural and grammatical features of the genre:

- it is written in the present tense;
- the sabotage procedure is sequenced chronologically in numbered steps;
- each instruction is preceded by a colon and begins with an imperative verb.

James had had no explicit teaching about the procedural genre. His only memories of written instructions were of those he had seen on a fire extinguisher and a Lego set 'but they were written differently'. As a voracious

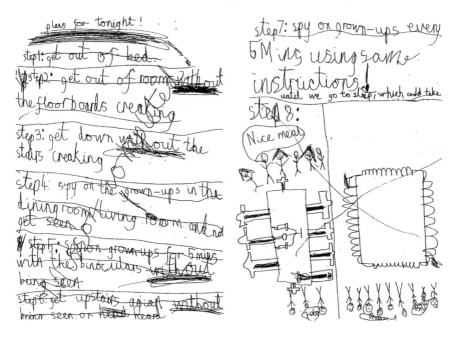

plans for tonight!

step1: get out of bed.

step2: get out of room without the floorboards creaking

step3: get down without the stairs creaking

step4: spy on the grown-ups in the dining room/living room and not get seen

step5: spy on grown-ups for 5 mins with the binoculars without being seen

step6: get upstairs again without being seen or being heard

Page 1

step7: spy on grown-ups every 5 mins using same instructions! until we go to sleep, which could take

step8:

Nice meal

Page 2

things to be aware of

all men at meal have good hearing!!!!!!!!!!!!!!!

floorboards and stairs do creak!

all grown-ups will have good sight!

Page 3

Figure 7.4:   James' plan

reader, however, he had probably absorbed procedural conventions unconsciously and could give a functionally accurate, if non-technical, explanation
of them. He did not, for example, know what a colon is, but was able to tell
me, 'It means *means!*' – a perfectly reasonable definition and, since this
writing enterprise was clearly meaning-driven, a particularly apt one.

Many children may lack the reading habits or capacity to ensure such
'natural' development. Need it follow, however, that explicit, structured
teaching methods must preclude children's personal motivation and playful
engagement? Research suggests that these elements are not simply desirable
but *essential* to high quality learning.

In Donaldson's (1978) seminal study of how children think and learn, she
showed how their capacity for conceptual understanding is fundamentally
determined by the degree to which learning is situated in meaningful
contexts. She warned of the danger of 'psychologically abstract' or 'cold-
blooded' tasks which are removed from 'all basic human purposes and
feelings and endeavours' when, in young children, 'the blood still runs warm'
(24). How teachers use language to present challenges to children is also
found to be a primary factor in facilitating thought processes:

> The primary thing is now held to be the grasp of meaning – the ability
> to 'make sense' of things, and above all to make sense of what people do,
> which of course involves what people say. On this view, it is the child's
> ability to interpret situations which makes it possible for him, through
> active processes of hypothesis-testing and inference, to arrive at a
> knowledge of language. (38)

Although she did not discuss Halliday's theory, Donaldson's view of the
relationship between thought and language learning would seem implicitly
to concur with a functional literacy pedagogy. Whatever the case for greater
specificity in the teaching of genres, respect for children's need to operate as
purposeful and meaning-driven users of language must remain at the heart
of all school-based learning. Accordingly this view should be integral to, not
separate from, the process of developing literacy. Because the three modes of
English are mutually supportive, language and literacy development cannot
be seen as discrete endeavours: children's school-based writing must be
informed by critically focused reading and discussion.

It should go without saying, but I fear it cannot, that the subject 'English'
– that contentious repository for political posturing – is intended to facilitate
human communication and understanding. Accordingly, progression in

English must be measured, not simply by the acquisition of discrete skills, but by children's ability to learn *through* and *about* language. Without this appreciation by teachers, it may be difficult to avoid a return to the transmission model of grammar teaching of the 1950s. If a pursuit of excellence lies behind the National Literacy Strategy, then such an outcome would surely be the ultimate irony.

8. Excellence in English and History: an arranged marriage or a love-affair?

Rosie Turner-Bisset

Introduction: what is excellence in teaching English through history?

Here is a puzzle for the reader. From the four vignettes presented below, which are examples of excellence in teaching English through history?

Vignette I

In the first classroom, a Year 2 class had just heard the story of Guy Fawkes. The teacher went into role as Guy Fawkes at the end of the story, and the children questioned the character as to details of his life, his part in the plot, and his reasons for doing it. The children were then given a facsimile of the Mounteagle letter, an anonymous letter sent to warn Lord Mounteagle of the danger in attending parliament on that day. They managed to decipher some of the seventeenth century writing, before being given a typed version. The teacher did not attempt to read the whole letter with them. Instead, she asked them to pick out any words which seemed to be serious or important. The children highlight-ed these words, finding 'danger,' 'your life' and 'terrible blow,' to give some examples. She asked them to hypothesise what the letter might be about. The children thought it might be a warning letter. She praised them liberally for their work on the text and their working out that it was a warning letter. She then read the whole letter to them, and they were able to uncover more of the meaning. The next activities were discussing the two versions of the Guy Fawkes story, with and without the letter, and experimenting with writing with quill pens to write their own warning letters. Finally the children acted out the story in an assembly, and explained to the school the importance of the letter in the story.

Vignette 2

In another school not far away, a Year 4 class were working on the Tudors. In a previous lesson they had made a timeline of Tudor monarchs and events such as the Armada, using topic books to help them place items at the right point on their timelines. This particular lesson was on Henry VIII, his marriages and the dissolution of the monasteries. The teacher had copied two double-page spreads from an attractively laid out book on the Tudors. Some pupils volunteered the rhyme: 'Divorced, beheaded, died, divorced, beheaded, survived' as a way of remembering what happened to each wife. They read the texts as a class, and answered some questions on a worksheet. These worksheets were pasted into the children's topic books on the Tudors. As an extension of this, some of the more able children wrote an account of what happened in their own words.

Vignette 3

Further along the corridor, a Year 3 teacher was tackling the Anglo-Saxons in Britain. She started by reading to the children a story from a commercially-produced history scheme: the story of Alfred the Great. When she finished it, she asked the children questions in order to establish their understanding, and asked them to write in their own words the story of Alfred. These stories were then placed in their history files. The next lesson started with the teacher showing a video about the Sutton Hoo Burial. The children watched with interest and there was some excitement over certain items of the finds from the burial site, especially the great shield and the helmet. After the video the teacher conducted a question-and-answer session on the content of it, and then gave the children the same questions to answer in written form. The next activity was drawing one of the treasures and writing a sentence about it to go on the class display.

Vignette 4

The final example is of a Year 5 teacher and the Romans in Britain. She considered that a key point in the history of Britain was the Boudicca rebellion. During it, power between Romans and Celts hung in the balance. It was also an exciting story. She got the class to move tables and chairs so that they were seated in a circle; then she told them the story of Boudicca up to the point where Seneca recalled the loan from the Iceni tribe. The main activity for the children was to conduct the council meeting of the Iceni to decide what to do about the loan. She allocated roles and all children were eager to play a part, including those with special educational needs. She explained the signals for commencing role-play and in role herself as chief elder, introduced the purpose of the council meeting. Gradually the less able boy, who had assumed the role of Boudicca, grew in confidence, listening to ideas, challenging them, inviting reluctant speakers and keeping order. Once ideas were exhausted, the teacher ended the role-play, gave a couple of minutes for relaxation, and then told the rest of the story. The follow-up activity was to write the story of Boudicca in their own words either in the third person or as a character in the story.

All these examples have been either observed or taught by the author. Only the first and last of these are examples of excellence in teaching either English or history. The second and third examples are, alas, all too common in English primary schools. They are presented as examples of weak or poor practice. Just because lessons involve some oral work, reading and writing, it does not mean that they reflect good practice in English. Likewise, because lessons involve aspects of English, using history as a vehicle for the practice of English skills, it does not mean that justice is done to either English or history. This chapter presents a rationale for judging excellence in teaching English through history. The rationale is based on an understanding of the nature of the disciplines of English and history, knowledge about how children learn, and a broad experience of teaching both English and history. Thus the rest of the chapter is structured as follows: the nature of history; the nature of English; background material on the arguments for integrating English and history; issues and possibilities in integration; children's learning; and concluding remarks on the four vignettes in relation to the rationale. History is dealt with first, if only because it is slightly less contentious a subject in the school curriculum, than is English.

The nature of history

The jury is still out as to the exact nature of history: indeed historians continue to debate this topic amongst themselves and in the national press (Evans and Munslow, 2001). However, a certain amount seems clear. History is the imaginative reconstruction of the past using what evidence we are able to find. We can state what we definitely know from the evidence. We can hypothesise or speculate about what we are unsure of. Finally, we can use other knowledge and evidence in order to interpret the evidence. Like other disciplines, history has substantive and syntactic structures (Schwab, 1978; 1964). The substantive knowledge of history has two aspects. First, there are the facts and concepts which comprise history, for example that Boudicca was the leader of the Iceni tribe; or concepts such as monarch, power, the church, trade and industry. There are also concepts peculiar to history such as the Middle Ages, the Blitz or the Reformation. Second, there are the organising structures or frameworks which help us to make sense of many disparate pieces of information. These include the over-arching concepts of history: chronology; a sense of period (historical situations); change; continuity; cause; effect; interpretation; and evidence. They also include paradigms, such as particular interpretations of history, which can guide enquiry, for example, Marxist or feminist paradigms. Syntactic structures are the processes by which new truths become established in a discipline. In history these are the skills and processes of historical enquiry: the searching for evidence; the investigation and interpretation of different kinds of evidence; recording of evidence; the interpretation and weighing of different sources and kinds of evidence; and the synthesis of historical narrative and argument. History is unlike science for example, in that evidence from the past is often incomplete or fragmentary. We hypothesise about the past using our imagination to 'fill in the gaps'. A useful conception of history is that of Trevelyan (1903), who saw it as a combination of three aspects: the scientific aspect of the systematic research through the surviving evidence base; the poetic/imaginative aspect, in the reconstruction of past events and lives; and the literary/artistic aspect in the communication of historical understanding.

This may seem far distant from the primary classroom but I would argue that a full understanding of the nature of history is essential for excellence in history teaching and for integrating history with any other subject such as English. The most common failing is a lack of knowledge and understanding about the syntactic structures of history. What tends to happen is that the children are taught historical content, without the processes of enquiry. The question: 'How do we know?' is not raised with children: thus teachers and children tend to treat the fruits of historical enquiry as given facts, rather than interpretations. History is then reduced to 'finding out' factual information from topic books, CD-ROMs, videos or the internet, without any true historical enquiry or consideration of the kinds of sources being used. In Schwab's terms, this is a corruption of the discipline. An attendant problem is the lack of understanding of substantive structures, of the over-arching concepts, such as primary and secondary evidence, or change and continuity. Thus the kind of evidence presented in topic books for example is not discussed. Often the pictures in topic books are primary evidence, whilst the bulk of the text is not. If primary teachers are aware of the distinction between forms of evidence, they can for example use the illustrations for enquiry, rather than as decoration. If teachers are not fully aware of the vast range of often difficult and abstract concepts in history, they can treat such words in texts as vocabulary to be defined, rather than ideas which need actively to be taught. Some of the problems described in this paragraph are present in Vignette 2 and 3.

How can teachers use ideas about the nature of history to inform their classroom practice? One of the most useful in terms of understanding history in the primary classroom is Hexter (1972). From him one can take the idea of 'doing history', meaning that we try to engage the children in tasks which have them acting as historians do. They follow the rules or syntactical structures of what historians do and understand how history differs from geography, science or English. Fines and Nichol (1997: 1) gave a very clear outline of doing history in the classroom:

- First, we must be examining a topic from the past and raising questions about it.
- Second, we must search for a wide range of relevant sources to provide evidence to help us answer our questions.
- Third, we must struggle to understand what the sources are saying (and each source-type has a different language) so that we can understand them in their own terms.
- Fourth, we must reason out and argue our answers to the questions, and support them with well-chosen evidence.
- Finally, we must communicate our answers for the process to be complete.

These processes can be seen as the rules of 'doing history'. Interpretation is central to the process of historical enquiry, as evidence can be viewed from a multitude of perspectives. There is a huge variety of remains from the past which can be used as evidence: archaeological remains, artefacts, pictures, photographs, paintings, engravings, cartoons, archive films, documentary evidence of all kinds, newspapers, magazines and books, diaries, memories, journals, eyewitness accounts, literature from a period, clothing, oral evidence, buildings and sites, the landscape and the environment, music, song and dance; even historical fiction and film are representations of the past. The task of children, acting as historians, is to collect, analyse, organise and interpret the evidence, weighing its validity against other evidence of the same event, person or period. In Hexter's (1972) terms the available sources are history's 'first record': the raw materials of primary sources and the secondary sources of interpretations of the evidence. In examining and interpreting these sources, or the 'first record,' we draw upon all our rich life experiences and knowledge up to that point. This wealth of experiences is what Hexter calls 'the second record'. It is usually private and personal, as well as individual. For example, a teacher's knowledge of Roman sites or passion for historical fiction would colour his or her interpretations of evidence from those periods. Another example might be of a child who knows only too well what divorce means in his or her family, bringing this experience to bear on the marital troubles of Henry VIII. Children do not have such broad and richly developed 'second records', as do adults: theirs are relatively unsophisticated, though they may have experienced many of life's troubles. In addition, children learn much history outside school through books, the media and visits to places of historical interest. The teacher's role is to extend their 'second records' by two means: through sharing his or her own 'second record' with them; and through providing opportunities for them to pool their knowledge through pair, group and whole-class discussion. Hexter's ideas of the first and second record are extremely valuable for understanding the processes of historical enquiry and informing teachers as they plan for teaching history. They can also partially illuminate our understanding of how children learn in history.

The nature of English

English is in a sense much more difficult to define than history. It is a broad church, not so much one discipline as a bundle of disciplines. It includes literature and language, literary criticism and linguistics. As a result, the nature of English is complex. In some senses it is a productive or creative discipline in the same way that art or music or design technology are: the processes of writing or composing poetry for example have something in common with creating a piece of art or music or technology. At the same time there is something of an enquiry element in the processes of literary criticism: the evidence in this case is the work of literature under examination. The reader or critic uses interpretation to inform judgements on, or responses to, the text. Those who study language employ some processes of enquiry, for example the use of language in a range of contexts and its relationship to culture and power. Thus English is problematical to define, being not one discipline, but several. Nonetheless there are concepts to be understood and used, for example: 'past tense', 'sentence', 'connective', 'verb', 'poem', 'story', 'letter', 'dialogue', 'genre' and 'autobiography', to name but a few. There are also facts, such as definitions of parts of speech, or genres of writing. Understanding of facts depends upon the understanding of the concepts of which they are composed. Over-arching concepts or paradigms are also present: for example, the guiding principles that language changes over time, or that as humans we use language primarily for social reasons, and for a multi-variety of purposes, can help us organise ideas about language and literature.

Perhaps because of the complexities in defining substantive and syntactic structures in a multi-disciplinary subject, it is more helpful to examine English as a school subject. Cox (1991: 17) pointed out how broad the subject was:

> It includes, for example, language use, language study, literature, drama and media education; it ranges from the teaching of a skill like handwriting, through the development of the imagination and of competence in reading, writing, speaking and listening, to the academic study of the greatest literature in English. Such broadness poses problems, both for the identity of English as a distinctive school subject, and for its relations with other subjects on the school curriculum.

He further helpfully listed five different views of the purposes of the teaching of English in schools, which he stressed were not to be regarded as 'sharply distinguishable' or 'mutually exclusive':

- a 'personal growth' view focuses on the child: it emphasises the relationship between language and learning in the individual child, and the role of literature in developing children's imaginative and aesthetic lives;
- a 'cross-curricular view' focuses on the school: it emphasises that all teachers (of English and of other subjects) have a responsibility to help children with the language demands of different subjects on the school curriculum: otherwise areas of the curriculum may be closed to them. In Britain, English is different from other school subjects, in that it is both a subject and a medium of instruction for other subjects;
- an 'adult needs' view focuses on communication outside the school: it emphasises the responsibility of English teachers to prepare children for the language demands of adult life, including the work-place, in a fast-changing world. Children need to learn to deal with the day-to-day demands of spoken language and of print; they also need to be able to write clearly, appropriately and effectively;
- a 'cultural heritage' view emphasises the responsibility of schools to lead children to an appreciation of those works of literature that have been widely regarded as amongst the finest in the language;
- a 'cultural analysis' view emphasises the role of English in helping children towards a critical understanding of the world and cultural environment in which they live. Children should know about the processes by which meanings are conveyed, and about the ways in which print and other media carry meanings and values.

(Cox, 1991: 21; adapted from original)

Ten years on from his work, it is true to say that at any one time, one or more of these five purposes predominates. At the time of writing, I would argue that the 'adult needs' view is in the ascendant, reflected in the concern with literacy, the introduction of the National Literacy Strategy and the drive to raise attainment in national tests. Whatever one's view of the literacy strategy, it is at least an attempt to empower all children, by equipping them with what they will need to make the most of life's opportunities and responsibilities. It is essential for teachers to be aware of these purposes, and to detect in the latest policy statements the underlying perception of the purposes of English in the curriculum. In terms of teaching English through history, all of these purposes are relevant: of greatest importance are the 'personal growth' aim and the 'cross-curricular' aim. English is both the way in which children can gain access to interpretation and understanding of historical sources, and the way in which they can communicate their understanding, through reading and writing, speaking and listening. Through the exercise of historical imagination, the wide range of historical sources can contribute to children's imaginative and aesthetic lives.

Integrating English and history

There is a considerable consensus that history and English are closely linked. Cooper (1992) stated that history was an umbrella discipline, incorporating all aspects of a culture. This would include its languages and literature, both spoken and written. Dean (1995: 10) argued that history was easily integrated with almost all subjects in the curriculum, but she added:

> No other subject however, is as compatible with history as English which fits history like a glove. The connection between history and English is far closer than a link: both are interpreted through language and concerned with language development; both are reading subjects; both explore people's feelings, conditions, motives, relationships; and both are concerned with understanding of the human condition.

Cooper (1995) discussed in particular the social dimension in language acquisition, arguing that discussion and group interaction contribute both to linguistic capability and historical expertise. Her research showed that history is an excellent context in which to develop discussion skills. Husbands (1996) pointed out that the nature of language is an important element in the teaching and learning of history. Nichol and Dean (1997: 82) claimed that all history teachers are teachers of language: the main ways of developing historical understanding are through speaking, reading and writing: 'History is a supremely literary subject, and the main source of historical information is the written word.'

Hoodless (1998) also saw language as an essential part of doing history. She pointed out that language and the use of English play an important part in any kind of historical activity, either at the level of the academic historian or at the level of a child working in a primary classroom. Nichol (1999: 78) further emphasised this in an article on literacy and history: 'Literacy is seminal to the learning of history, for history is a particular kind of discourse with its own conventions, idioms and vocabulary.'

I added my own voice to the consensus (Turner-Bisset, 2001). In an article describing a case study exploring the links between history, literacy and music, I argued that history is a literary subject, following Trevelyan's conceptualisation of history as a combination of three aspects: the scientific aspect, the poetic/imaginative aspect, and the literary/artistic aspect. One of the key elements of history (DES, 1995; DfEE/QCA, 1999) is the organisation and communication of ideas, information and historical understanding: this is the most obvious literary element of history, although the other key elements all involve some literary activity.

Issues and possibilities in teaching English through history

Despite the strong consensus about the links between English and history, there are nonetheless certain issues and concerns which require discussion. There is a concern that history specialists have rushed to embrace the idea of teaching history and English together in order to preserve the place of history in the primary curriculum. The first issue is that both English and history should be genuinely represented by what activities are planned for the classroom. In other words, in both subjects, the tasks given to children to promote learning should reflect the nature of the discipline. This means in history that the processes of historical enquiry, and interpretation using primary evidence should be included (as they frequently are not) as an integral part of lesson planning, teaching and assessment. In English the nature of the discipline is more complex, but learning activities should reflect the importance of the fact that language and literature are about meaning. In the TTA-funded study of effective teachers of literacy (Medwell *et al.*, 1998), it was argued that effective teachers of literacy believed that the creation of meaning was fundamental in the teaching of English. Teachers' under-pinning beliefs about literacy, communication and meaning had some impact on the effectiveness of their teaching. Thus, while there are strong links between English and history, the nature of each subject is different, as are the aims of studying them in the primary curriculum. In planning for teaching English through history, this can present problems. The most immediate issue is whether two different sets of lesson objectives can be reconciled within the same lesson or scheme of work.

This question has been raised by teacher educators and beginning teachers alike. Cooper and Twistleton (1998a) worked on a project with students and teachers to explore the possibilities of teaching the literacy hour as an integral part of work on a history project. The difficulty lay in taking the learning objectives of the literacy hour and using them as a basis for planning genuinely historical activities. They described feeling very constrained by both the termly format of the literacy framework (DfEE, 1998) and by the requirement to work at word, sentence and text level (Historical Association Workshop, 1998). Nonetheless, some excellent teaching was done by students and teachers in the project, using for example, Victorian alphabet books with Year 2 and Year 5 classes, as well as museum visits, artefacts and photographs (Cooper and Twistleton, 1998b). Nichol (1999) described some of the approaches of the Nuffield Primary History Project in teaching literacy and history to a Year 3 class, showing work at word, sentence and text level through an investigation of a body in a bog. Hoodless (1998) presented a range of examples of teaching history and English across Key Stage 1 and 2. Turner-Bisset (2001) showed how history, English and music could be combined to produce high-quality extended writing in a Year 6 class. However, despite all the curriculum development work done in this area, the key issue of different sets of objectives remains.

As part of a research project on the beliefs and practice of beginning teachers of a four-year B.Ed. course learning to teach history, I interviewed thirteen student-teachers at the end of the course about their final teaching practice. All of the students except two reported being heavily constrained by the expectations of the school and teacher. History was used as a vehicle for teaching English, but only in the narrow sense of using topic book texts as comprehension passages. The students placed in Year 2 and Year 6 in particular found that history was seen as an opportunity to practise for the standard assessment tests. It is likely that both the pressure of the tests in English and an ignorance of the nature of history, particularly the processes of enquiry, contributed to this kind of weak practice in history lessons. One student reported that her Year 2 children had to produce writing before they were allowed to draw anything or do any other activity. Another was placed in a Year 2 class in a school which taught literacy through all subjects of the curriculum. The teaching approach, which she had to follow, was to use 'big books' on history topics such as Christopher Columbus to teach the content. Her view on this reflects some of the inherent problems:

> 'I must say that I don't feel I taught history ... The school actually had literacy taught across the curriculum, and although I feel that you can teach history and literacy, I feel that it is quite a difficult task, and you have to be very focused on what you actually want them to do. I feel that

the school is pushing the literacy objectives more than the history ones; so I felt that wasn't really teaching history, but more literacy … although I conformed and learnt a lot from it, I feel that you have to be much more careful when it is cross-curricular: it has to be appropriate. You have to be clear on what you want them to learn. I found that really hard particularly if I had one literacy objective and one history objective. Although the children would achieve those, I felt it was too much to ask of them because they tried to focus on literacy and history, and that's too much for them. They need to be focused.' (Sarah, final year B.Ed. student)

There is a central tension between the requirements of the two subjects. It is certainly true that if one has too many learning objectives for a lesson, one can lose the focus of the intended learning outcome. On the other hand, it is clear that by limiting oneself to one history and one English objective, these can be achieved. Perhaps the most important points arising from this issue are the need for a deep understanding of the nature of each subject; the ability to analyse both history and English curricula and determine the content and aspects which map on to each other and to be aware of this central tension.

Having discussed some of the issues, we may move on to the possibilities. The value of history in the teaching of English is that it provides a meaningful context for the learning, practice and development of knowledge, skills and understanding in English. The content of history is endlessly fascinating: it is first and foremost about people, relationships and events, and often expressed in narrative forms. Children doing real history, in Hexter's terms, are able to investigate the past and exercise their considerable curiosity. History provides opportunities for discussion, children asking questions, drama, role-play, and a wide variety of texts for reading, and colourful material for children to develop imagination and produce writing in a range of genres. The contributions history can make to the different aspects of English, speaking and listening, reading and writing, are considered in turn.

Speaking and listening

In engaging children in genuine historical activities, the opportunities for speaking and listening are abundant. Storytelling is a wonderful and sometimes neglected teaching approach, across the curriculum, but especially so in English and history. Telling a story as opposed to reading means that the teacher 'creates' the story in the telling. It makes possible eye contact with the class, the use of movement, gesture, space, voice and body language: in short all of the non-verbal channels of communication as well. Storytelling can be used as an economical way to teach ideas and information about a period of history. For example, in the story of Guy Fawkes, the children can learn about daily life in seventeenth century England, the use of tinder boxes and lanterns, how the Houses of Parliament were heated, and that there were no cameras or television. This can be done much more effectively through storytelling than through research in topic books. Moreover, children seem to retain information more easily and for longer periods from a story. Perhaps it is true that humans are programmed to listen to stories, as a way of making meaning, and this way of making sense of the world is so innate as to function extremely powerfully as a method of teaching. Stories engage and fire the imagination and can provide material for the children's own writing. A further exciting aspect of learning through stories is that they aid concept development and the learning of vocabulary through the repeated hearing of words in a context. To take Vignette 1 again, the story of Guy Fawkes is generally considered appropriate for Key Stage 1, but contains difficult concepts such as 'Protestant,' 'Catholic,' 'Parliament,' and 'treason.' Through the storytelling children can begin to have some understanding of these concepts, because they occur several times within a meaningful context.

Drama can be used in a variety of ways to enhance children's sense of period and understanding of historical situations and to develop their imagination. The 'hot-seating' technique used in Vignette 1, in which children question the teacher (or one of their peers) in role as a historical character, is extremely useful. It enables children to ask the questions, rather than the teacher; it extends understanding, particularly of difficult areas such as the power of religious beliefs and of human motives ('Guy Fawkes, do you honestly think you are doing the right thing?') and the children get the opportunity to explore ideas through spoken language before putting pen to paper. Other forms of drama also offer some of these advantages. In Vignette 4, the same approach of storytelling and drama was used, but this time the teacher paused in the story and the children took the action forward through the device of the Iceni council meeting. The semi-formality of the council meeting provided opportunities for all children to speak in role in a meaningful context, to engage with the difficulties facing the Iceni tribe at that point in time and to listen to other children's contributions. In terms of inclusion and catering for a range of educational needs, both storytelling and drama are powerful ways of enabling all children to gain access to knowledge, skills and understanding. After such teaching children are 'fired-up' to write, often using a range of interesting vocabulary choices.

The value of discussion has already been mentioned (Cooper, 1992). In examining for example a collection of artefacts, children use a range of adjectives to describe them, and debate the possible function of unfamiliar objects. Teachers and children alike can extend each other's 'second record' (Hexter, 1972) by drawing on experiences outside the classroom to explain artefacts. The social interaction of pair and small group work on a collection of artefacts or on pictures can facilitate learning and language development through peer interaction (Vygotsky, 1978). Presenting findings or interpretations to the class in pairs helps children to pool knowledge; in doing so they are using language to express themselves and to explore ideas.

Reading

History requires critical reading of texts, as does English. Although historical evidence comes in a huge variety of forms, one main form of evidence is the written word, in the form of documents of all kinds. In history we need to ask ourselves what sort of a document we are examining, who produced it, for what purpose, for what kind of audience and in what context. These questions are equally relevant to English. Documents provide a huge range of texts upon which one can draw for the literacy hour. They can be very challenging. Dean (1995: 10) argued that history is the most demanding literacy subject on the curriculum: 'in no other subject will children encounter texts using as many long words, new words and difficult grammatical constructions.' The role for the teacher is to make documents accessible to all the class. This can be done in several different ways. One way is through active whole-class teaching, as in Vignette 1. The teacher deliberately asked the children not to try to read the whole document, but to look for certain words and phrases. This enabled them to scan for words they recognised; words which were serious or important. All children were able to read something in the letter. By sharing what they had read in the whole-class setting other children could come to understand the purpose of the letter. Only after skimming and scanning activities did the teacher read the whole letter with plentiful expression to aid communication of meaning. This approach can be used on a wide range of documents. Another way is to generate an example of the genre of document with the children. For a lesson involving census returns, the teacher can demonstrate the headings and get the children to make their own entries to create a class census. Only then would the teacher bring out the 1851 census for the area. The children are then familiar with the headings and able to tackle the difficult text. This approach involves the generic principle in children's learning of starting where the children are and working towards the unfamiliar. Texts can also be adapted, to make them easier to read (but it does mean that an extra layer of selection and interpretation is involved through the teacher's translation of the original text), or preferably tape-recorded, so that children can listen to as well as read the words, or listen instead of reading, depending on their reading ability. Another method is to cut a document into short sections, the children working in pairs on a section each, then pooling their understanding of each bit of text in a whole-class plenary. Children should be invited to question texts, rather than the teacher always asking the questions, for questioning is an important historical process; in language terms, the children can focus on what they do not understand and ask for clarification. Text-marking is extremely useful for highlighting and extracting information; if this is combined with the use of grids to record and organise information, the basis of a piece of extended writing in whatever genre is already established.

Writing

The last point brings us to writing. History provides a superb context for a range of writing activities. Those presented in Vignette 2 and 3 represent the weakest and least imaginative practice in teaching English through history, being mainly comprehension and recount activities. History is useful for sorting out ideas; pursuing enquiries; asking questions; tabulating inform-ation on grids; and making lists, for example of items the children can see in a picture. For more extended pieces of work, it is useful for noting evidence; tracing developments over time; drafting arguments; making statements; writing descriptions and constructing narratives. In addition, children can write from someone else's perspective and in a vast range of genres, as befits a context in which the written evidence itself is available in a huge range of genres. Husbands (1996) gave a comprehensive list of genres for writing in history, which he called 'The Writing Generator' (Figure 8.1). Even this list is not exhaustive, and readers may think of other genres which would be appropriate within a historical context for developing skills in writing. The important points to remember are the twin functions of writing within a historical context: to explore ideas and organise information; and writing to

acknowledgement	gloss	poster
advertisement	graffiti	prayer
affidavit	greetings card	precis
announcement	guide	proclamation
article	headline	prospectus
autobiography	horoscope	questionnaire
ballad	instruction	recipe
biography	invitation	record
blurb	journal	reference
brief (legal)	label	report
broadsheet	letter (various types)	resume
brochure	libel	review
caption	list	rule
cartoon	log	schedule
catalogue	lyric	script
certificate	magazine	sermon
charter	manifesto	sketch
confession	manual	slogan
constitution	memo	song
critique	menu	sonnet
crossword	minutes	specification (job)
curriculum	monologue	spell
curriculum vitae	news	statement
definition	notes	story
dialogue	notice	summary
diary	novel	syllabus
directory	obituary	synopsis
edict	pamphlet	telex
editorial	paraphrase	testimonial
epitaph	parody	travelogue
eulogy	placard	weather forecast
feature	play	will
forecast	poem	
form	postcard	

Figure 8.1:   The Writing Generator (Husbands, 1996: 113)

communicate our interpretation and understanding to an audience. In relation to Hexter's model of doing history, these would be the stages of struggling to understand what the sources are saying (which of course involves reading as well) and reasoning using the evidence; then communicating our answers to an audience. That communication can be in a huge range of genres of writing (the symbolic form) in pictures (the iconic form) and in action, such as drama and role-play (the enactive form).

Children's learning

There is not space in this chapter for a detailed consideration of children's learning, but I would argue that some ideas about how children learn are essential for the successful teaching of English through history. The most useful set of theories comes from Bruner (1970) in his idea of there being three characteristic ways of understanding the world. He argued that we form mental representations of everything we encounter in the real world, and that there are three forms of mental representation: enactive representation or understanding by doing; iconic representation, or understanding through pictures, maps and diagrams; and symbolic representation, or understanding through symbol systems, such as language, mathematical notation or musical notation. Young children tend to use enactive modes first, then iconic, and finally symbolic forms. Adults move back and forth between all three forms of representation in achieving and expressing understanding. It follows that we need to give children learning experiences which reflect all three forms of representation, including drama and role-play, drawing and painting as well as reading and writing. Concepts, of which there are so many in history, and which provide an extended vocabulary, can be taught using any of the three modes of representation. Thus 'authority' could be taught by means of a brief role-play in which the teacher told off a previously briefed child and sent her out. I have used this approach myself in teaching about power and authority in Tudor times: the activity which followed of making rules and discussing which were good and bad rules, enhanced the children's understanding of law and power. The rule-making involved a short piece of writing which was then shared with the class and discussed.

The other set of ideas, already mentioned in passing, came from Vygotsky (1978). The notion of the zone of proximal development is helpful. This is the potential for learning, understanding and doing which is not yet realised, but which can be realised through interaction with others. This social interaction which helps children to achieve with others what they may not be able to achieve on their own, can either be in whole-class discussion, or in pair and small-group work. Children can pool their ideas, test them against each other and enhance their understanding. In Hexter's terms, they are extending their second records through interaction with the teacher or with each other. For example, the children in the Year 2 class in Vignette 1 were helped in their understanding of what it means to be a Catholic, by one child from that faith talking about it. The ideas of Bruner and Vygotsky can inform our planning for teaching English through history. In particular we need to plan to use a variety of teaching approaches which enable children to learn language through history.

Conclusion

It is now possible to justify why Vignette 1 and 4 are examples of excellent practice, and why Vignette 2 and 3 are not. In Vignette 1, the teacher used a variety of teaching approaches, including enactive and symbolic forms of representation in the storytelling, drama, hot-seating, reading documents, and writing. Discussion was extensively used with the whole class. The activities reflected the enquiry processes of history, yet provided reading and writing activities within an authentic setting. The teacher in Vignette 4 also used storytelling and drama, discussion and writing to teach about Boudicca. The children learnt concepts and vocabulary such as 'invasion', 'rebellion', 'slaughter', 'loan,' 'battle formation', and 'chariot'. Rosen (1993) has written extensively about the value of storytelling and the children writing their own version of the story immediately afterwards. The story and drama enabled the children to 'take possession' of the historical information and to communicate their understanding in vivid pieces of writing. In this case the story was based on the evidence of Tacitus, a Roman historian. Both of these lessons showed a good understanding of the nature of both English and history, and of the importance of the historical context for providing authentic situations for speaking and listening, reading and writing.

By contrast, Vignette 2 and 3 are examples of weak practice. The activities are not genuinely historical in that there is no investigation of primary evidence, no engagement of the historical imagination, and rather dull reading and writing activities. In Vignette 2, the activities reflect an approach to history as English comprehension, without any consideration of how children learn. Frequently the purpose of these kinds of lessons is to produce a topic book containing writing on many different aspects of content. There is no understanding of historical processes in this lesson. To use history in this way, as a practice ground for English comprehension, is poor practice indeed. In Vignette 3, the teacher read the story of Alfred rather than telling it, a practice less likely to engage the children's interest or promote understanding and learning. Video, as in this example, is frequently used as a form of text, and used for comprehension-style questions, rather than for other purposes. For example, after the video, the children could have investigated A4 size pictures of the treasures, by which they were excited, and used them to say what they knew about the Anglo-Saxons from the things that were buried at Sutton Hoo. Writing could have been in the form of lists of points from the evidence, later re-drafted into longer archaeologists' reports. Finally the emphasis on producing work for display, whilst not necessarily a bad thing, meant that less attention was paid to the children's learning in either English or history.

In summary, to achieve excellence in teaching English through history, one needs: a deep understanding of the nature, purpose, content, skills and processes of the two subjects; some knowledge of how English and history might be integrated; an informed understanding of how children learn; and a broad pedagogical repertoire, which includes a wide range of teaching approaches. Otherwise, English and history are likely to be more of an arranged marriage than a love affair.

Notes on Contributors

Judith Ackroyd is senior lecturer in drama at University College, Northampton where she contributes to drama and teacher training courses. After teaching in two schools she worked as an advisory teacher for drama delivering in-service courses for teachers. She has published widely in the field of drama education. She is co-author of *Drama Lessons for 5-11 years olds*, and author of *Literacy Alive: drama projects for literacy learning*.

Jo Boulton is senior lecturer in primary education at University College, Northampton where she teaches English on the BA QTS course. She has taught in lower and primary schools in Northamptonshire and worked for Northamptonshire Inspection and Advisory Service as a curriculum adviser for English and drama. She is the co-author of *Drama Lessons for 5-11 Years*.

Melanie Bradley is senior lecturer in professional English at the University of Central England in Birmingham. She has taught in primary and infant schools, during which time she was an English co-ordinator. Her main research interest is the development of linguistic and literary knowledge in primary-aged children and their teachers.

Mark Brundrett is programme leader for the MBA in educational management at the University of Leicester and a visiting professor at the University of Hertfordshire. Prior to working in higher education he taught in secondary, middle and primary schools and was, for five years, a headteacher.

Kathy Caddy is headteacher at Killigrew Junior School in St Albans, Hertfordshire. Prior to this she was English co-ordinator, deputy and then acting headteacher at Redbourn Junior School, Hertfordshire.

Diane Duncan is research leader in the education department of the University of Hertfordshire where she teaches English to student teachers. She has researched and published in the area of mature student teacher socialisation and is the author of *Becoming a Primary Schoolteacher*. She has been a primary school teacher and headteacher of three schools.

Kate Hirom has taught English in schools for over twenty years. She has worked for the Open University on both PGCE and postgraduate courses and was a teacher associate on the Shakespeare and Schools Project. She has led in-service sessions for teachers on active approaches to Shakespeare and on multicultural literature and is at present researching ways in which drama can improve writing in the primary school. She is currently senior lecturer in the school of education at University College, Northampton.

Tim Parke has taught across the maintained sector, in language schools and in ESOL (English for speakers of other languages) classes. He is in the department of linguistics at the University of Hertfordshire, teaching second language acquisition and contributes to teacher education programmes. His research interest is in the language development of bilingual children.

Fred Sedgwick, freelance lecturer and writer, specialises in children's writing, art and personal, social and moral education. He is also author of *Shakespeare and the Young Writer* and is currently working on a new book *Children Learning through Drawing*. His latest book is *Teaching Literacy: a creative approach*.

Peter Silcock is visiting professor of education at the University of Hertfordshire. He has worked for many years in teacher education, most recently as a senior research fellow at De Montfort University. He is Chair of the Association for the Study of Primary Education.

Rosie Turner-Bisset is senior lecturer in primary history education at the University of Hertfordshire. She is a member of the Nuffield Primary History Project team and teaches history, literacy and IT across Britain on in-service courses. Her research interests include teaching and learning, curriculum matters, beliefs and practices of teaching history and the full range of topics concerning professional development.

References

Ackroyd, J. (2000) *Literacy Alive: classroom drama for literacy learning*. London: Hodder and Stoughton.

Ackroyd, J. and Boulton, J. (2001) *Drama Lessons*. London: David Fulton.

Arnold, S. (2000) "Bang to rights", *The Observer*, 30th April.

Baker, P. and Eversley, J. (eds.) (2000) *Multilingual Capital*. London: Battlebridge.

Barnes, D. (2000) *Becoming an English Teacher*. Sheffield: NATE.

Barnes, D. (1976) *From Communication to Curriculum*. Harmondsworth: Penguin.

Barnes, D. and Sheeran, S. (1992) "Oracy and genre: speech styles in the classroom" in K. Norman (ed.) *Thinking Voices: the work of the National Oracy Project*. London: Hodder and Stoughton.

Barnes, D., Britton, J. and Rosen, H. (1969) *Language, the Learner and the School* (revised edn). Middlesex: Penguin Books.

Barthes, R. and Sontag, S. (eds.) (1982) *A Barthes Reader*. London: Cape.

Beard, R. (1999) *National Literacy Strategy Review of Research and Other Related Evidence*. London: HMSO.

Benton, M. and Fox, G. (1985) *Teaching Literature Nine to Fourteen*. Oxford: Oxford University Press.

Bhatt, A. and Martin-Jones, M. (1992) "Whose resource? Minority languages, bilingual learners and language awareness" in N. Fairclough (ed.) *Critical Language Awareness*. London: Longman.

Bloom, H. (1998) *Shakespeare: the invention of the human*. London: Fourth Estate.

Bloomfield, L. (1933) *Language*. London: Allen and Unwin.

Bolton, G. (1979) *Towards a Theory of Drama in Education*. London: Longman.

Booth, D. and Neelands, J. (1998) *Writing in Role*. London: Caliburn Press.

Boshell, S. (2000) "Giant steps in writing" in J. Ackroyd (ed.) *Literacy Alive*. London: Hodder and Stoughton.

Boulton, J. (2000) "A brighter colour for the literacy hour" in J. Ackroyd (ed.) *Literacy Alive*. London: Hodder and Stoughton.

Brown, R.W. (1973) *A First Language: the early stages*. Cambridge, MA: Harvard University Press.

Brundrett, M., Duncan, D. and Smith G. (2001) "Re-creating the 'Virtuous Circle': new directions in the teaching of English" in M. Brundrett, D. Duncan, and P. Silcock (eds.) *The Primary School Curriculum*. Dereham: Peter Francis.

Bruner J. (1970) "The course of cognitive growth" in B.L. Klintz and J. Brunig (eds.) *Research in Psychology*. New York: Scott, Foresman and Co.

Bullock, A. (1975) *A Language for Life*. London: HMSO.

Chambers, A. (1985) *Booktalk: occasional writing on literature and children*. London: The Bodley Head.

Chukovsky, K. (1963) *From Two to Five*. San Francisco, CA: University of California Press.

Clipson-Boyles, S. (1998) *Drama in Primary English Teaching*. London: David Fulton.

Coleridge, S.T. (1974) *Biographica Literaria*. London: Penguin.

Cooper, H. (1995) *The Teaching of History in the Early Years*. London: David Fulton.

Cooper, H. (1992) *The Teaching of History*. London: David Fulton.

Cooper, H. and Twistleton, S. (1998a) "Literacy and history". A paper presented at the Historical Association Annual Conference, Manchester.

Cooper, H. and Twistleton, S. (1998b) "Victorian alphabets: a sampler for the literacy hour?", *Primary English Magazine*, 4, 2: 7-11.

Cox, B. (1995) *Cox on Cox*. London: Hodder and Stoughton.

Craft, M. and Atkins, M. (1985) *Training Teachers of Ethnic Minority Community Languages* (A report for the Swann Committee). Nottingham: University of Nottingham School of Education.

Currie, L.N. (1997) "Why use a novel?", *Reading*, April, 11-16.

Dean, J. (1995) *Teaching History at Key Stage 2*. Cambridge: Chris Kington Publishing.

DES (1998) *National Literacy Strategy Training Materials Module 5*. London: DES.

DES (1995) *History in the National Curriculum*. London: HMSO.

DES (1992) *The Implementation of the Curricular Requirements of the Education Reform Act: English Key Stages 1, 2 and 3. A report by HM Inspectorate on the second year 1990-91*. London: HMSO.

DES (1990) *Language in the National Curriculum (LINC): materials for professional development*. London: HMSO.

DES (1989) *English for Ages 5-16* (The final Cox Report). London: Department of Education and Science and the Welsh Office.

DES (1988) *The Report of the Committee of Enquiry into the Teaching of the English Language* (Kingman Report). London: HMSO.

DfEE (2001) *The National Literacy Strategy: shared writing on school placement. Key Stage 1 and Key Stage 2*. London: DfEE.

DfEE (2000) *The National Literacy Strategy: grammar for writing*. London: DfEE.

DfEE (1998) *The National Literacy Strategy: framework for teaching*. London: DfEE.

DfEE (1997) *Excellence in Schools*. London: HMSO.

DfEE/QCA (2000) *English in The National Curriculum for England*. London: HMSO.

DfEE/QCA (1999) *The National Curriculum for England: history*. Norwich: HMSO.

Dixon, J. (1987) "The question of genres" in I. Reid *The Place of Genre Learning: current debates, no 1*. Centre for Studies in Literary Education, Deakin University: Typereader Publications.

Donaldson, M. (1989) *Sense and Sensibility. Some thoughts on the Teaching of Literacy*. Reading: Reading and Information Centre, University of Reading.

Donaldson, M. (1978) *Children's Mind*. Glasgow: Fontana Press.

Duncan, D. (1999) *Becoming a Primary School Teacher: a study of mature women*. Stoke on Trent: Trentham Books.

Eccleshare, J. (2001) "The proliferation of modern 'Classics'", *Books for Keeps*, 126, 1: 3-5.

Evans, R. and Munslow, A. (2001) "Facts to fight over", *The Guardian*, 6th February.

Fines, J. and Nichol, J. (1997) *Teaching Primary History*. Oxford: Heinemann.

Fisher, M. (1991) "Surprise sandwiches", *Books for Keeps*, 7, 1: 53-84.

Foster-Cohen, S.H. (1990) *The Communicative Competence of Young Children: a modular approach*. London: Longman.

Fowlie, W. (ed.) (1956) *Journals of Jean Cocteau*. London: Routledge.

Foreman, M. (1972) *Dinosaurs and all that Rubbish*. Harmondsworth: Puffin Books.

Frater, G. (2000) "Observed in practice. English in the NLS: some reflections", *Reading*, 34, 3: 107-10.

Freire, P. (1987) *Literacy: reading the world and the word*. New York: Bergin Garvey Inc.

Gleason, J. and Berko, M. (eds.) (1989) *The Development of Language* (2nd edn). Columbus, OH: Merrill.

Goodz, N. (1994): "Interactions between parents and children in bilingual families" in F. Genesee (ed.) *Educating Second Language Children*. Cambridge: Cambridge University Press.

Graham, L. (1999) "Changing practice through reflection", *Reading*, 33, 3: 228-33.

Gray, M. (1984) *A Dictionary of Literary Terms*. London: Longman.

Gregory, E. (1996) *Making Sense of a New World: learning to read in a second language*. London: Paul Chapman.

Gregory, R.L. (1974) "Psychology: towards a science of fiction", *New Society*, 23rd May.

Hall, N. and Robinson, A. (1994) *Keeping in Touch Using Interactive Writing with Young Children*. London: Hodder and Stoughton.

Halliday, M.A.K. (1975) *Learning How to Mean: explorations in the development of language*. London: Arnold.

Halliday, M.A.K. (1973) *Explorations in the Function of Language*. London: Edward Arnold.

Hardy, B. (1968) "Towards a poetic of fiction: an approach through narrative", *Novel: A Forum on Fiction*.

Heath, S.B. (1983) *Ways with Words: language, life and work in communities and classrooms*. Cambridge: Cambridge University Press.

Heath, S.B. (2001) "Pictures: art, narrative and childhood". Paper presented at Reading International Symposium, Homerton College, Cambridge.

Heathcote, D. (1979) *Drama as a Learning Medium*. Lewes, Sussex: Falmer Press.

Hedberg, N.L. and Westby, C.E. (1993) *Analyzing Story-Telling Skills: theory to practice*. Tuscon, NZ: Communication Skills Builders.

Heras, A.I. (1994) "The construction of understanding in a sixth-grade bilingual classroom", *Linguistics and Education*, 5: 275-99.

Hexter, G.H. (1972) *The History Primer*. London: Allen Lane.

Hill, W. and Ottchen, C. (1991) *Shakespeare's Insults*. Cambridge: Mainsail.

Hirst, K. (1998) "Pre-school literacy experiences of children in Punjabi, Urdu and Gujerati speaking families in England", *British Educational Research Journal*, 24, 4: 415-29.

Hoff-Ginsberg, E. (1997)"Frog stories from 4-year-olds: individual differences in the expression of referential and evaluative content", *Journal of Narrative and Life History*, 7, 1: 223-7.

Hoodless, P. (ed.) (1998) *History and English in the Primary School: exploiting the links*. London: Routledge.

Husbands, C. (1996) *What is History Teaching: language, ideas and meaning in learning about the past*. Buckingham: Open University Press.

Hynds, J. (1998) "Will there be any time left for reading?", *Books for Keeps*, 110: 146-57.

Janes, E. (2001) *Contexts of Meaning: assessing bilingual pupils' comprehension of text* (Report of a project funded by the Teacher Research Grant Scheme). London: Teacher Training Agency.

Kempe, A. and Lockwood, M. (2000) *Drama in and out of the Literacy Hour*. Reading: Reading and Language Information Centre, University of Reading.

Kitson, N. and Spiby, I. (1995) *Primary Drama Handbook*. Birmingham: Questions/Watts Books.

Knapp, P. and Watkins, N. (1994) *Context-Text-Grammar: teaching the genres and grammar of school writing in infants and primary classrooms*. Melbourne: Text Productions Australia.

Kress, G. (1987) "Genre in a social theory of language: a reply to John Dixon" in I. Reid (ed.) *The Place of Genre Learning: current debates, no 1*. Centre for Studies in Literary Education, Deakin University: Typereader Publications.

Laskey, M. (1999) *The Tightrope Wedding*. Huddersfield: Smith/Doorstop.

Lewis, M. and Wray, D. (1995) *Developing Children's Non-fiction Writing: working with writing frames*. Hove: Scholastic.

Levis, N. (2001) "The brave new world of bilingual teaching", *The Times Educational Supplement*, IV-V, 2nd March.

Lezard, N. (2000) "A wreath for the Reith Lectures", *The Independent on Sunday*, 30th April.

Lubach, P. (1992) *Donald and the Singing Fish*. London: Macmillan.

Magorian, M. (1981) *Goodnight Mister Tom*. Harmondsworth: Penguin Books.

Mast, G. and Cohen, M. (eds.) (1974) *Film, Theory and Criticism: introductory readings* (1st edn). New York: Oxford University Press.

Medway, P. (1990) "Into the sixties: English and English society at a time of change" in I. Goodson, and P. Medway (eds.) *Bringing English to Order*. Lewes: Falmer Press.

Medwell, J., Wray, D., Poulson, L. and Fox, R. (1998) *Effective Teachers of Literacy* (A report of a research project commissioned by the Teacher Training Agency). Exeter: University of Exeter.

Meek, M. (1988) *How Texts Teach what Readers Learn*. Stroud: Thimble Press.

Moffett, J. (1968) *Teaching the Universe of Discourse*. London: Houghton Mifflin.

Moss, E. (1997) "Classic cuts", *Books for Keeps*, 110: 126-33.

Neelands, J. (1993) *Writing in Imagined Contexts*. Toronto: Research Services, Toronto Board of Education.

Neelands, J. (1992) *Learning Through Imagined Experience*. London: Hodder and Stoughton.

Neelands, J. (1984) *Making Sense of Drama*. London: Heinemann.

Neelands, J. and Goode, T. (2000) *Structuring Drama Work: a handbook of available forms in theatre and drama*. Cambridge: Cambridge University Press.

Nias, J., Southworth, G. and Yeomans, R. (1989) *Staff Relationships in the Primary School*. London: Cassell Education.

Nichol, J. (1999) "Murder! literacy and history", *Reading*, 33, 2: 78-86.

Nichol, J. and Dean, J. (1997) *History 7-11: developing primary teaching skills*. London: Routledge.

Norman, K. (ed.) *Thinking Voices: the work of the National Oracy Project*. London: Hodder and Stoughton.

O'Neill, C. (1995) *Drama Worlds*. Portsmouth, New Hampshire: Heinemann.

O'Neill, C. and Lambert, A. (1982) *Drama Structures: a practical handbook for teachers*. London: Stanley Thornes.

OFSTED (1999) *The National Literacy Strategy: an evaluation of the first year of the National Literacy Strategy* (A report from the Office of Her Majesty's Chief Inspector of Schools). London: OFSTED Publications Centre.

Oldham, J. (1999) "The book of the film: enhancing print literacy at KS3", *English in Education*, 33, 1: 36-45.

Paley, V. (1981) *Wally's Stories*. Cambridge, MA: Harvard University Press.

Parekh, B. (ed.) (2000) *The Future of Multi-ethnic Britain* (Report of the Commission on the future of multi-ethnic Britain). London: Profile.

Parke, T.H. (2001) "Words and turns: bilingual and monolingual children construct a story", *Linguistics and Education*, 12, 4: 409-30.

Parke, T.H. and Drury, R. (2001) "Language development at home and school: gains and losses in young bilinguals", *Early Years* 21, 2: 117-27.

Parker, D. (1999) "You've read the book, now make the film: moving image media, print literacy and narrative", *English in Education*, 33, 1: 24-9.

Perera, K. (1984) *Children's Writing and Reading*. Oxford: Oxford University Press.

Pinker, S. (1994) *The Language Instinct: the new science of language and mind*. Harmondsworth: Penguin.

Pirrie, J. (1987) *On Common Ground*. London: Hodder and Stoughton.

Pound, E. (1954) *Cantos*. London: Faber.

Powling, C. (1991) "Classic variations", *Books for Keeps*, 7, 1: 32.

QCA (1998a) *Standards at Key Stage 1 English and Mathematics. Report on the 1998 National Curriculum Assessments for 7-Year-Olds*. London: QCA Publications.

QCA (1998b) *Standards at Key Stage 2 English and Mathematics. Report on the 1998 National Curriculum Assessments for 11-Year-Olds*. London: QCA Publications.

Roberts, N. (1998) *The Integrated Literacy Hour 1*. Wisbech St Mary: Nicholas Robert Publications.

Robinson, K. (1999) *All Our Futures: creativity, culture and education* (A report by the National Advisory Committee on Creative and Cultural Education). London: DfEE.

Rosen, B. (1993) *Shapers and Polishers: Teachers as Storytellers*. London: Collins Educational.

Rosen, C. and Rosen, H. (1973) *The Language of Primary School Children*. London: Penguin.

Scholes, R. (1985) "Narration and narrativity in film" in G. Mast and M. Cohen (eds.) *Film Theory and Criticism: introductory readings* (3rd edn). New York: OUP.

Schwab, J. (1978) "Education and the structure of the disciplines" in I. Westbury and N.J. Wilkof (eds.) *Science, Curriculum and Liberal Education*. Chicago: University of Chicago Press.

Schwab, J.J. (1964) "The structure of the disciplines: meanings and significances" in G. Ford and L. Purgo (eds.) *The Structure of Knowledge and the Curriculum*. Chicago: Rand McNally.

Sedgwick, F. (2001) *Teaching Literacy: a Creative Approach*. London: Continuum.

Sedgwick, F. (2000a) *Jenny Kissed Me*. Birmingham: Questions Publishing.

Sedgwick, F. (2000b) *Forms of Poetry*. Dunstable: Belair.

Sedgwick, F. (1999) *Shakespeare and the Young Writer*. London: Routledge.

Shakespeare, W. (1999) *Coriolanus* (Rex Gibson edn 1999). Cambridge: Cambridge University Press.

Shakespeare, W. *King Lear* (Elspeth Bain, Jonathan Morris and Rob Smith edn 1996). Cambridge: Cambridge University Press.

Shakespeare, W. *Romeo and Juliet* (Rex Gibson edn 1984). Cambridge: Cambridge University Press.

Shakespeare, W. *Troilus and Cressida* (Rex Gibson edn 1984). Cambridge: Cambridge University Press.

Shakespeare, W. *Love's Labour's Lost* (R.W. David edn 1968). London: Routledge.

Silcock, P. (2001) "What is excellent teaching?" in M. Brundrett, D. Duncan and P. Silcock (eds.) *The Primary School Curriculum*. Dereham: Peter Francis.

Slade, P. (1954) *Child Drama*. London: University of London Press.

Squire, J.R. (1964) *The Response of Adolescents while Reading Four Short Stories*. Champaign, Illinois: NCTE.

Squire, J.R. and Applebee, R.K. (1969) *Teaching English in the United Kingdom*. Sheffield: National Council of Teachers of English.

Stubbs, M. (ed.) (1985) *The Other Languages of England*. London: Routledge.

Sutherland, J. and Watts, C. (2000) *Henry V, War Criminal and Other Shakespeare Puzzles*. Oxford: Oxford University Press.

Tarone, E. and Liu, G-Q. (1995) "Situational context, variation, and second language acquisition theory" in G. Cook and B. Seidlhofer (eds.) *Principles and Practice in Applied Linguistics*. Oxford: Oxford University Press.

Trevelyan, G.M. (1903) "Clio, a muse", *Independent Review*, December.

Turner, M. (1991) "Finding out", *Support for Learning*, 6: 28-32.

Turner-Bisset, R.A (2001) "Serving-maids and literacy: an approach to teaching literacy through history and music", *Reading*, 35, 1: 27-31.

Vendler, H. (1997) *The Art of Shakespeare's Sonnets*. Cambridge, Massachusetts: Belnap Press.

Vygotsky, L.S. (1978) *Mind and Society*. Cambridge, MA: Harvard University Press.

Vygotsky, L.S. (1962) *Thought and Language*. New York: Wiley.

Wagner, B.J. (1979) *Drama as a Learning Medium*. London: Hutchinson Books.

Warlow, A. (1977) "What the reader has to do" in M. Meek, A. Warlow and G. Barton *The Cool Web*. London: The Bodley Head.

Watson, V. (1991) "What makes a children's classic?", *Books for Keeps*, 7, 1: 218-24.

Way, B. (1967) *Development through Drama*. Longman: Harlow.

Wells, G. (1987) *The Meaning Makers*. London: Hodder and Stoughton.

Wells, G. (1986) *The Meaning Makers: children learning language and using language to learn*. Portsmouth: Heinemann Educational Books.

Wells, G. (1992) "The centrality of talk in education" in K. Norman (ed.) *Thinking Voices: the work of the National Oracy Project*. London: Hodder and Stoughton.

Wells, S. (1978) *Shakespeare: an illustrated dictionary*. London: Kaye and Ward.

Whitehead, M.R. (1997) *Language and Literacy in the Early Years*. London: Paul Chapman Publishing.

Winograd, P. and Johnston, P. (1987) "Some consideration in advancing the teaching of reading comprehension", *Educational Psychology*, 22: 213-30.

Woolland, B. (1993) *The Teaching of Drama in the Primary School*. London: Longman.

Wordsworth, L. and Roberts, J. (1999) "Read any good films lately?", *English 4-11*, Summer: 10-12.

Wray, D. and Medwell, J. (1998) *Effective Teachers of Literacy*. Exeter: Exeter University.

Zentella, A.C. (1997) *Growing up Bilingual: Puerto Rican children in New York*. London: Blackwell.

Index